SOLUTION-FOCUSED STRESS COUNSELLING

Titles in the *Stress Counselling* Series

Ellis, Gordon, Neenan and Palmer, *Stress Counselling: A Rational Emotive Behaviour Approach*
Milner and Palmer, *Integrative Stress Counselling: A Humanistic Problem-Focused Approach*
Palmer and Dryden (eds), *Stress Management and Counselling: Theory, Practice, Research and Methodology*
Scott and Palmer, *Trauma and Post-traumatic Stress Disorder*

STRESS COUNSELLING SERIES

SOLUTION-FOCUSED STRESS COUNSELLING

Bill O'Connell

CONTINUUM
London and New York

Continuum
The Tower Building, 11 York Road, London SE1 7NX
370 Lexington Avenue, New York NY 10017–6503

www.continuumbooks.com

First published 2001

British Library Cataloguing-in-Publication Data
A catalogue record for this book is available from the British Library.

ISBN 0 8264 5312 0 (hardback)
0 8264 5311 2 (paperback)

Designed and typeset by YHT Ltd, London
Printed and bound in Great Britain
ByTheCromwellPress

Contents

Acknowledgements

I would like to acknowledge the influence of Bill O'Hanlon, Steve de Shazer, Insoo Kim Berg and Yvonne Dolan, whose ideas have inspired and challenged me, as they have challenged many thousands of others. I would like also to thank all my students and clients who continue to teach me so much. I would like to thank my colleagues at the University of Birmingham Westhill who made the writing of this book possible. In particular my thanks go to my closest colleague Janet Bellamy and to Marian Jordan for her help. Thanks to Martin Lawn for encouraging me to write in the first place, to Alan Clark for sharing ideas, to Caroline Jones for her support, to Bebe Speed, my supervisor, from whom I have learnt a great deal, to Steve Conlon and Harry Norman for their generous sharing of ideas and contacts, to Stephen Palmer, my editor, for his belief in me and in the book and to Joanne O'Connell for her proofreading and ideas for improving the text.

A big pat to Annie our dog who supervised me on many long vigils in front of the computer and whose insistence on being taken for walks helped me to contain my stress levels. Without constant love, support and encouragement from my wife Moira and three grown-up daughters, Donnamarie, Joanne (the real writer in the family) and Katrina, this book would never have seen the light of day.

Foreword

The aim of this series is to focus on different approaches to stress counselling and management. It is intended that the books will link theory and research to the practice of stress counselling and stress management. Leading counselling, clinical and occupational psychologists, biologists, counsellors and psychotherapists will report on their work, focusing on individual, group and organizational interventions.

The books will interest both undergraduate and postgraduate students as well as experienced practitioners in the helping professions, in particular those who work in the fields of counselling, psychology, psychotherapy, sociology and mental and occupational health.

This book, *Solution-Focused Stress Counselling,* is the fifth book in the *Stress Counselling* Series. The need and desire for brief forms of therapy has increased in recent years. Solution-Focused stress counselling, by its very nature, is intrinsically brief. As soon as counselling starts, it cuts to the chase by focusing on solutions and avoids becoming hindered by problems. It is an approach that is ideally suited to the stress counselling arena.

Professor Stephen Palmer
City University and Centre for Stress Management, London

Preface

This book presents a new model of stress based upon Solution-Focused Therapy (SFT). The model, which emerged from the USA in the 1980s, has been well received in Europe where it now has a sizeable following among caring professionals. The book will interest practitioners who are open to new ideas and who want to broaden their own repertoire of interventions with clients. The book does not claim SFT is superior to any other therapies, although some of the recent converts to it make extravagant claims on its behalf and can sound as if they have found the one true faith. It is true that it differs from conventional models and challenges some of the sacred cows of therapy, but the spirit of this book is inclusive and integrative with Chapter 6 in particular being a bridge between the therapies.

Chapter 1 outlines how the solution-focused approach to stress counselling differs from a problem-focused one. Taking a solution-focused perspective gives both the client and the counsellor a different way into resolving the problem. Since 'nothing always works' most hard-pressed counsellors welcome any useful ideas which serve the interests of their clients. Although the founders of the approach worked within a family therapy setting, the approach has also been used with groups, couples and individuals in a wide variety of settings. It belongs within the brief therapy tradition which is particularly apposite today in an era of time-limited work. The book sets out the key structural and process characteristics which make it more likely to be a catalyst for change. At the same time we need to recognize that the contribution model-specific elements make to client change is less crucial than the impact of the therapeutic relationship. Techniques need to be used within the context of a sound therapeutic relationship. The chapter also outlines an agenda of solution-focused skills.

In Chapter 2 the theoretical foundations of the solution-focused model are examined. Epistemology – the philosophy of knowledge – is a critical area for therapists who engage in very specialized forms of language games. How language is used in therapy and the practical consequences of unacknowledged epistemological positions is addressed in this chapter. For readers whose priority it is to plunder models for new interventions without subscribing to the ideas behind them, this chapter could be safely skipped in favour of those which immediately follow. However, the gap between research, theory and practice does not serve the therapy profession well, and by-passing the theory is not an effective long-term strategy. This chapter also offers the reader a solution-focused model of stress.

Chapters 3, 4 and 5 describe the solution-focused process. They identify and explain the key interventions used by the counsellor. Chapter 6 establishes a dialogue with other therapeutic approaches. It acknowledges the limitations of the solution-focused model but also suggests what its strengths might be and how these could be integrated into the work of practitioners committed to working eclectically. Chapter 7 applies the model to couples and groups and offers an outline programme for a stress management group. Chapter 8 focuses on the organizational dimensions of stress and how the solution-focused approach might be useful at this level. A model for solution-focused reflecting teams is described.

I hope the book will serve the cause of solution-focused therapy because it is my conviction, based on my own counselling practice, that it has much to offer hard-pressed practitioners and clients. Its respect for clients' individuality and dignity stirs my soul at all times. Its imaginative questions clearly touch parts of the client which have not been used or recognized for a long time, if at all. As long as it does not become a cult, nor its 'big names' gurus, it has much to teach us all.

For Moira my wife and Donnamarie, Joanne and Katrina my daughters, who made all the difference.

CHAPTER 1

The Foundations of Solution-Focused Stress Counselling

INTRODUCTION

Solution-focused counselling is a form of brief counselling which builds upon clients' resources. It aims to help clients to achieve their preferred outcomes by evoking and constructing solutions to their problems. It challenges the traditional problem-focused orthodoxy of most other approaches. With clients suffering from stress it maximizes their resources and abilities and helps them to remember what they have always known, but have temporarily forgotten. It is revolutionary because clients teach the counsellors how they can be helpful and the counsellors trust the clients to teach them. The work together is strongly collaborative. It is as egalitarian as a relationship in which one person occupies a vulnerable role can be.

The solution-focused approach conflicts with some other therapeutic traditions so it is worth noting how Perry (1970) describes competition between conflicting philosophies. He argues that individuals may respond to conflict in different ways:

- **Dualists** who believe that one school of thought is right or true and the others are false or wrong.
- **Multiplists** for whom diversity and uncertainty is a legitimate but temporary stage of development. They believe at some stage one school or theory will be proven correct and come out on top.
- **Relativists** for whom diversity and uncertainty are not temporary phases because all knowledge is contextual and relative. The most one can ever say is that it is 'true' for these people at this point in time.

The philosophy behind solution-focused counselling is relativist (see Chapter 2).There are already many different strands within the solution-focused school, such as Possibility Therapy, Solution-oriented Therapy, Post-modern Therapy and Narrative Therapy. Although they differ they belong to the same family. They stand in opposition to therapies influenced by the medical model or to the ones which see the therapist as an expert. To those trained in the more traditional therapies, some of the followers of these new therapies, with their enthusiasm and evangelical spirit, can appear to be dismissive of what has been learnt about helping people in distress over the past 100 years. My own preference is not in a single school of therapy as the answer to the world's problems but in a broader approach integrating ideas and practices from many different therapies and giving a pivotal position to solution-focused values. It contrasts with some followers of post-modern/social construc-tionist schools such as Neuro-linguistic Programming, Narrative Therapy or Solution-oriented Therapy, who, in their allegiance to 'the faith' and dedication to their leaders, show some of the marks of a sect or cult of zealous, smug and intolerant 'true believers'.

SOLUTION THERAPY

Clients report problems because there is a gulf between the demands of their immediate environment and their perceived ability to cope with them. Inevitably, their 'reports' omit to recognize those areas of their lives which are more part of the solution than part of the problem. Their 'problem stories' lack breadth or depth and offer them limited perspectives on solutions. These unfinished and unbalanced stories can lead the client to adopt unrealistic rules for living which cause stress. For example, 'I must never make mistakes and if I do it will be a disaster'. These partial and distorted narratives support a limited repertoire of behaviours, such as working ever harder to make a job secure. In order for the client to break out of this vicious circle, he or she needs to bring other stories about themself back into their consciousness. The solution-focused approach encourages clients to develop positive self-narratives about their resources and competence.

The term 'solution' does not imply that for every problem in life there must be a solution if only we could find it. As Rabbi Kushner (1986) in his exploration for meaning puts it, 'There is no Answer, but there are answers'. Most often the 'solution' to a problem is an accumulation of small solutions, pieces of a solution jigsaw puzzle. Solutions are the building blocks of change – they are how people create meaning in their lives. When these elements – which obviously vary from person to person – are active, people feel more alive and fulfilled. A solution-focused approach does not prescribe what these elements might be – they are defined by the client and form their agenda for change. Berg and De Jong (1996) describe solutions for clients as 'changes in perceptions, patterns of interacting and living, and meanings that are constructed within the client's frame of references' (p. 377). Providing the client's goals are legal, moral and ethical, the counsellor honours and stays close to them. The counsellor respects the client's unique way of creating solutions.

In solution-focused conversations solutions and component parts, by which I mean exceptions, goals and resources, are brought to the forefront of the client's reality. The client is helped to contact aspects of himself which have been buried under the oppressive weight of stress in his life. Connecting with solutions in the here and now becomes an experiential event witnessed by the counsellor. So counselling becomes not just a journey back into the mists of time to locate the lost origins of problems but a search to recover lost solutions and resources. Some of these may come from the client's own unique history, others may come from his cultural heritage. Cultures with strong oral traditions will have a rich collection of 'solution stories'. Problems are uncompleted solutions. People who withdraw under stress have made a start in recognizing and dealing with a situation they perceive as a problem but it is an inadequate solution. Those who drink to cope with their exhaustion have acknowledged their problem and have begun to deal with it, although their starter for a solution may become more part of the problem than part of the solution. A solution-focused approach will look out for signs that people have begun to address their problems. Where possible it will help them to expand or modify them until they become effective solutions.

Even the search for solutions itself can be overdone. Armstrong (1999) comments:

> I believe that an overemphasis on finding solutions is misplaced, with the idea of solutions taken literally to mean 'escaping from distress'. While it is human to want to be happy, my experience as a therapist tells me that much of the distress in people's lives is often largely inescapable. In my view it is often more helpful to help clients to construct or discover meaning in their distress; to come to some personal understanding about what this means for them, and, perhaps to answer the question: why me? (p.16)

FOCUSED THERAPY

As with all therapies, the counsellor edits the material the client brings, in this case by focusing upon solutions, goals and client resources. In order to maintain this focus there is a disciplined structure which anyone claiming to be solution-focused needs in broad terms to follow. This process will be explored in detail later in Chapter 3.

All forms of counselling have a structure, even those which claim not to have one. Their structure may be more hidden but is still there. The counselling contract is based upon clients wanting counsellors to assume an influential role in their lives. Once contact is established it is impossible for the counsellor to avoid being influential. The only choice is in the direction of the influence. The solution-focused practitioner consciously chooses to exercise influence over the client by co-generating new understandings and strategies which the client has not yet either developed or implemented.

There is a sense of direction and forward movement in solution-focused interventions. This keeps the client's goals clearly in focus. Continuity with the client's agenda is maintained through a process of mutual evaluation and review. The counsellor aims not to create change but to discover where change is occurring and to cooperate with the client in expanding it. A fundamental assumption made in the solution-focused approach is that the client has already begun to act in ways which are helpful in achieving his goal. No matter how grim the situation, the client is doing some things right, although not enough of them to alleviate the problem. Rather than believe the counsellor's role is to discover alternative strategies for the client, the counsellor focuses upon what the client has already demonstrated he can do. The counsellor seeks to help the client to find ways of extending his repertoire of solutions. Since the emphasis is on future-oriented solution conversation, the problem agenda is limited. There is no need to look for 'underlying' issues. The presented problem is regarded as a gift from the client and becomes the focus of the work.

BRIEF THERAPY

A consensus definition of brief therapy would be under twenty sessions (this sounds like long-term therapy for a solution-focused counsellor, who will see most clients for far fewer sessions than that). There is considerable agreement in the literature about the main characteristics of planned brief therapy. Barrett-Kruse (1994, pp. 109-15) summarizes these as:

- the view that self and others are essentially able
- the acceptance of the client's definition of the problem
- the formation of the therapeutic alliance
- the crediting of success to the client
- the therapist learning from the client
- the avoidance of a power struggle with the client
- the objectification rather than the personalization of the client's behaviour.

She asserts that in brief therapy the therapist needs to join with the client to communicate an expectancy of change. For her, this necessitates a mixture of cooperation and directiveness from the therapist to enable a working relationship to form as quickly as possible. Most writers stress how important it is to identify the problem and the goal(s) clearly and to develop carefully evaluated action plans. In brief therapy the client negotiates a definition of the problem with the counsellor. In emphasizing the need to educate clients into their roles, Wells and Gianetti (1993) argue a collaborative and effective relationship can be more quickly established if clients are given as much information as possible about the problem and the therapy. Solution-focused counsellors actively work at demystifying the therapeutic process by explaining to clients the rationale for the approach and the interventions being used. Solution-focused counselling belongs to the brief therapy tradition associated with Milton Erickson (1980), John Weakland *et al.* (1974) and members of the Mental Research Institute at Palo Alto, California. It differs from time-limited therapy which stipulates a specific number of sessions available to the client. In the solution-focused tradition, brief means an ethical commitment to work economically, simply and efficiently with minimal intrusion into the client's life. For brief counselling to be effective, the counsellor needs to believe that it is qualitatively different from long-term work, not inferior to it but different. Since, in practice, most therapy is brief (Koss and Butcher, 1986), irrespective of which model is used, the solution-focused approach cannot claim brevity as its core value. However, there are elements in the approach which increase the probability that the therapy is more likely to be brief than long term. These are shown in the box below.

Box 1.1 *Keeping the brief in brief therapy*

Restrict the amount of historical investigation
Attend to the client's goals
Work on what is right rather than what is wrong
Give clients honest and uninhibited positive feedback
Designate clients as the experts in their own lives
Focus on solutions not problems
Evaluate and attend to ending

ORIGINS

The Brief Family Therapy Team in Milwaukee, Wisconsin, USA, led by Steve de Shazer (de Shazer *et al.*, 1986) were the founding members of Solution-focused Therapy. De Shazer himself maintains that credit for the clinical development of the model belongs to his colleague and wife, Insoo Kim Berg. He felt his contribution was to codify the theory and practice (de Shazer, 1999). The team observed that by engaging their clients in conversations about their preferred futures, they were equally effective in making changes as when they took time and care to explore the history of the 'problem'. Clients appeared to be very interested in describing what they wanted to happen in their lives. These descriptions of what their solutions would look like sometimes related directly to the problem but often did not. The solutions emerged without reference to the problem but were closely connected to the elicited goals of the client. Once the clients were able to articulate their solutions they often saw the original problem in a different light. As the focus on the solutions grew the attention on the problem receded.

The team discovered, moreover, solutions could be evoked from clients by the skilful use of certain future-oriented questions. This led to de Shazer (1985) and his colleagues developing standard interventions ('skeleton keys') which could be applied whatever the presenting problem. They argued it was not essential to understand how a lock operated to use the key to open the door. These keys included: seeking exceptions to the problem; getting the client to 'do something different'; the use of scaling; the miracle question; the taking of one small step and the giving of therapeutic compliments.

Their central concern was pragmatic and simple – what worked for this client? They encouraged clients to work on what was changeable and attainable. They took a sceptical attitude to the labels the clients or their referrers attached to themselves. They chose instead to suspend judgement about the problems while focusing upon the clients' non-problem behaviour, competences and personal strengths.

SOLUTIONS NOT PROBLEMS

There are significant differences between a problem-focused and a solution-focused approach.

Problem-focused approach	*Solution-focused approach*
From problem	To solution
Past	Future
Causes	Multiple descriptions
Why?	How?
Insight/cure/growth	Change
What happened?	What do you want?
Deep	Surface
Counsellor led	Collaborative
What is wrong?	What is right?
Client learns from counsellor	Counsellor learns from client
Long and painful	Brief and need not be painful
Treatment fits problem	Solutions fit person
Expert language	Utilizes a client's frame and language
Resistance	Cooperation

The dynamics of the relationship, the purpose of the conversation and the assumptions and values behind both approaches are different.

PROBLEMS OR SOLUTIONS

This is not really an either/or but a both/and. The difference lies in the proportion of time allocated to problem talk and that allocated to solution talk. The problem-focused therapist sets out to elicit as much knowledge and understanding as possible about the stress described by the client. In contrast, the solution-focused therapist builds a detailed picture of what the client's solutions might look like. Clients typically become more interested in what their solutions look like and how they could come about than in the nature of the stress problem they brought with them. As they explore solutions they may also begin to frame the problem in a different way.

PAST AND FUTURE

Of course the past is crucially important in our understanding of ourselves in the present. We are who we are, at least in part, because of who we have been but we are also who we are because of who we want to be in the future. We invest time and effort today because of our hopes and dreams for tomorrow. In counselling it is not always necessary or helpful to start with the client's history. Starting with what the client wants can be more productive. Young people, in particular, are more willing to invest time in finding out what they could become than in what has gone before. Knowing how to get the life you want is often more attractive than working out how you got the one you have. The speed of social and technological change and the short shelf life of much knowledge means our understanding of the past will often fail to help us know how to tackle the future. Egan (1998) sums up how counsellors might use the past:

If the past can add clarity to current experiences, behaviours and emotions, provide clues as to how self-defeating thinking and behaving can be changed now, let it be discussed. However, if the past becomes the principal focus of the client's exploration, helping is likely to lose the name of action.   (p.128)

CAUSES OR MULTIPLE DESCRIPTIONS

The problem-focused therapist facilitates the client's exploration of his or her past in order to develop with them a rationale for their current stress. There is an expectation that if together they can make connections, see patterns or links between past events and present behaviour, then the client will be able to use this learning to make changes. For the solution-focused therapist the past can only be reconstructed from a present perspective. It cannot be recovered or discovered. If a client's history is a catalogue of problems, exploring new ways of understanding and behaviour from a future perspective, rather than an historical one with its negative associations, can be more helpful. This does not mean it is unimportant for individuals to experience empathy and acceptance from the counsellor. Most therapies aim to help clients to move beyond their existing life story to develop one which will open up new possibilities for living.

WHY OR HOW?

'Why do we behave as we do?' contrasted with 'How could we behave as we want?' The former emphasizes the need to get behind or underneath the client's reality, to find out what the unconscious or other factors might be which have created the problem. The latter takes the view that there are many answers or explanations for problems and no way of knowing which is 'right' or 'true' but only which fits/works for a particular individual at a certain point in time. The 'Why' question takes us into the realms of speculation and inference. It appeals to the intellect. It invites rational logical thinking. The 'How' question leads us into descriptions of what actually happens in very specific and concrete ways.

EXAMPLE

Counsellor: Why do you think you are depressed?

Client: My father and my sister were both depressed, I suppose I inherited it in my genes.

Counsellor: How else do you explain it to yourself?

Client : I was ill when I was small and had to stay in hospital for almost a year. I recently read in a magazine that children who were separated from their parents when they were small had problems attaching to them when they came home. I wondered if that is why I am depressed.

Counsellor: I understand. What other things have you been thinking about?

Client: I have recently left an abusive relationship where my partner was always criticizing me and undermining my confidence.

Three quite distinct lines of enquiry have been opened here. One sees the depression as biologically inherited, another sees it as a result of early childhood experiences and a third as related to a recent damaging relationship. The depression may be associated with all three experiences or with none, or with these and others not yet identified (society will gladly offer many others if required).

For the solution-focused practitioner, the more crucial issue is how the client uniquely experiences depression and whether he or she can give an operationalized description of it.

EXAMPLE

Client: I stay in bed all day. I have got no energy for anything. I have become quite isolated, I put everyone off. I am irritable and miserable a lot of the time. I have lost all interest in my hobbies. I sit and watch daytime television and I am sleeping a lot to escape my partner who is always complaining that I do nothing to help.

INSIGHT/CURE V CHANGE

In a sense all counselling is educative. This is true insofar as it aims to bring the client from an existing point of knowledge, feeling and action, to one which enables him to see his situation in a different light. The only question is, therefore, how this learning comes about. From the psychodynamic standpoint, for example, learning comes through the client with the active help of the therapist:

* reflecting upon the experience of the therapeutic relationship (transference)
* owning the interpretations of conscious and unconscious material
* being able to make connections between past and current events
* integrating and testing out discoveries.

Learning in the solution-focused way is somewhat different. It happens mainly when the counsellor helps the client to enrich her current descriptions/explanations imbedded in the narrative of her life by including resources, strengths and exceptions to the problem. This learning takes place not so much in the session itself or in the relationship between counsellor and client but more in the 'world out there'. There is a strong orientation to the client's context for living. The client is encouraged to discover truths about himself by making experiments in testing out new attitudes and actions. Insight need not come in verbal communication but from consciously chosen action followed by reflection and evaluation. As Heaton (1972) writes: 'Insight is developed by reflection on experience, and the more passionate the experience the deeper the insight.' Lomas (1987:135), in discussing the above, refers to this experience as primarily the relationship between the therapist and the client. However he also warns against imposed insights which imply that 'change occurs simply by means of increasingly convincing intellectual presentations' (p. 56). If it is the case that there are different learning styles (Honey and Mumford, 1992) then experiential learning will appeal to and work for some people more than others.

Activists, who learn by doing and whose motto is 'I'll try anything once', will be more enthusiastic and successful in learning from tasks given to them than reflectors – who like to stand back and weigh up experiences from different angles before committing themselves. They need time and sufficient information to think through issues to their intellectual satisfaction before they will act. They may be more convinced if there is a well-crafted rationale for their problems and for the proposed solutions. Others, whose dominant learning style is pragmatic, will be likely to take to new ideas if they are clearly practical. Theorists, on the other hand, like to analyse and synthesize ideas. Their detached intellectualism may lead to a cautious approach to experimentation. A good counsellor will adapt to fit clients with different problem-solving styles. It is the solution-focused way to give clients choices and to cooperate with them in whichever way seems most helpful.

WHAT HAPPENED? V WHAT DO YOU WANT?

Clients invariably want to tell the counsellor something about how they came to be so stressed. They may have strong ideas about who is responsible for the amount of stress they are suffering. There may be a lot of unfinished business relating to it. At some point, however, all clients have to choose how they are going to move forward in the light of all that has gone before. These pivotal moments are likely to arise more often in a form of therapy which majors on future-oriented questions. It may be that the constant rhythm of these questions can bring people to this point of resolution sooner than those therapies which devote more time to discussions about the client's history. It is at the moment when the client is ready to contemplate seriously the kind of short- and long-term future which they want, that solution talk becomes extremely useful. It provides an avenue for escaping the downward spiral of problem talk.

DEEP V SURFACE

Be profoundly superficial. A. Boyd (1999) *Life's Little Deconstruction Book*

Consistent with the philosophy underpinning the model (see Chapter 2) the counsellor stays with the surface material the client brings. This material is not considered to be superficial or symptomatic of something deeper.

COUNSELLOR LED V COLLABORATIVE

In some forms of therapy the counsellor clearly occupies a leading and directive role. In the cognitive-behavioural tradition the counsellor takes an instructional, educative role; in the psychodynamic tradition the counsellor occupies the expert role offering interpretations of the client's material. In the solution-focused approach the counsellor works to a structure which excludes interventions which are problem focused. At the same time the solution-focused counsellor adopts a 'not knowing' role in which he or she abdicates the role of expert and becomes a companion on a journey 'in contrast to therapies which diagnose, prescribe, and then seek to manoeuvre, enlighten, or change the client or family to reach these prescribed goals, the brief therapist is more easily seen as an ally' (Washburn, 1994: 50). Abandoning the expert role does not mean the counsellor lacks expertise. If the counsellor lacked counselling skills/theoretical knowledge/ethical awareness, she would be guilty of incompetence and unprofessional practice. Counselling/psychotherapy bodies operate licensing and accreditation schemes to ensure that professionals work within their competence and practise ethically. The professionalization of counselling which has accompanied such regulatory bodies is not without its disadvantages however. One disadvantage is that it can widen the gap between the counsellor and the client. In highlighting the skills, knowledge and experience of the counsellor, it can deskill clients and undermine their confidence in their own resources.

WHAT IS WRONG V WHAT IS RIGHT

Some therapies focus upon the client's problem history, their deficits, their pathology, their problem patterns, their unresolved issues and their unfinished business. At times it can seem as if not much of the client is functioning well. The emphasis in the solution-focused approach is the opposite. It is on what is *right* not *what is wrong*; what *works* not on what *does not work*; on what the past has taught or given you, not on how it has weakened you; on strengths not weaknesses; on what you can do, not on what you cannot do.

CLIENT LEARNS FROM COUNSELLOR V COUNSELLOR LEARNS FROM CLIENT

There is a mutuality of learning in the solution-focused approach. The counsellor is a guest in the client's life, the client can be trusted to find out how to make use of the counsellor. If the counsellor is attentive, the client will show him how to be an effective counsellor with her. When the counsellor suspends his belief about knowing what the problem is or what the solution might be, he can ask questions which bring forth the client's innate but possibly under-utilized wisdom. This willingness to accept the client at face value so to speak does not mean the counsellor is gullible or naïve. But it contrasts with the mindset which characterizes the following passage:

> As surely as the client seeks help for himself by coming into counselling he will also place obstacles in the way of this help ... The client will seek to establish a spurious sense of intimacy or mutuality from early on in the relationship ... They appear rational and cooperative and appear to take an intelligent interest in their counselling. Having come into counselling they spend their time trying to avoid becoming a client ... Basically the client's wish is to prevent the counsellor from functioning as a counsellor, to prevent her from thinking about the client and so stop her understanding him.   (McLoughlin, 1995: 41)

LONG AND PAINFUL V BRIEF AND NOT NECESSARILY PAINFUL

Some therapies assume for the process to be effective it needs to be lengthy and painful for the client. When examined more closely, these assumptions are often based on nothing more substantial than guesswork, cultural influences and expectations. Why should long-term therapy be predicated *a priori* for a client? Should it be on the grounds of the severity of the problem, its duration, the extent of the client's support network or their level of motivation? There is inadequate research evidence to support the accuracy of such judgements. In fact the weight of research is all in the other direction – in favour of assuming the therapy will be brief unless the case is made out to the contrary (summarized in Koss and Butcher, 1986). There is no intrinsic necessity for counselling to be painful. It might be but it may also be exciting, fun, amazing and intriguing. How painful does it have to be to be effective? Does it have to be painful at all? This is not advocating a therapy without tears but it is questioning assumptions of what must happen in therapy for it to be effective. A solution-focused view would be that nothing *has* to happen in therapy but that all sorts of things *may* happen. What happens is negotiated between the two parties at the time and cannot be forecast in advance. Anecdotal evidence suggests humour, for example, figures highly in solution-oriented sessions.

TREATMENT FITS PROBLEM V SOLUTION FITS PERSON

Detaching the solution process from the problem process logically leads to the axiom that *the solution needs to fit the client not the problem*. As a consequence, the counsellor will want to find out about the whole of the client's life not just the part of it which is problematic. A holistic view of the person is likely to yield more positive solutions than one which takes only a limited interest in non-problem aspects. Given the rich variety of human beings the range of solutions to problems is endless. All clients are evolutionary successes who have adapted to their environment and have overcome thousands of problems to do so.

EXPERT LANGUAGE V UTILIZES CLIENT'S FRAME AND LANGUAGE

Some therapies mystify the counselling process by the use of intellectualized jargon. This chess game of words does not take place on a level playing field since only one person knows the language rules of the game. A solution-focused conversation, by contrast, sounds very ordinary and down-to-earth, there is an absence of technical expressions and abstract words. As Washburn (1994) states:

> Therapy is not for everyone, but some therapy is for more people than others. Insight oriented therapy, or therapy which interprets interpersonal processes to achieve change tends to be utilised by bright, motivated people, often with higher education and professional experience. (p. 51)

A solution-focused approach employs and encourages conversations which are grounded in the client's day-to-day realities. These conversations do not include speculations about the *causes* of problems but do include speculation about possible *solutions*.

RESISTANCE V COOPERATION

A solution-focused understanding of resistance is that it is a form of non-cooperation from the client. It is designed to convey to the counsellor there is a mismatch between what the counsellor is doing and what the client needs at the moment. It is a signal to do something different such as speed up, slow down, be more empathic, listen more, move on or talk more.

CORE COUNSELLING SKILLS

Solution-focused concepts are not difficult to grasp but to effectively implement them an appropriate use of skills common across the therapies and ones specific to the model is required. The following is a list of common core skills although some counsellors might not subscribe to all of them.

Box 1.2 *Core counselling skills*

Active listening – being fully engaged and tracking the client's story.
Affirmation – You have shown a lot of courage in what you've had to fight against.
Before and after questions – You said that last Christmas was a low point for you, what was life like for you before then?
Brainstorming – working with the client to generate as many possible options as possible.
Challenging client's thinking – What's the evidence that you are a failure because you're finding it difficult to make a long-term relationship?
Completing client's sentence – (use sparingly)
Empathy (Basic) – So you feel confused and torn in different directions.
　　　　　　　(Advanced) – I wonder if you're really feeling that it was all your fault although you've been told that it wasn't.
Evaluating – asking the client whether the work together is proving helpful. Reviewing progress or lack of it.
Exploring images – So does it look to you as if this mountain can be climbed by different routes or only one?
Giving information – In panic attacks people sometimes feel their hearts racing, they may begin to hyperventilate ...
Goal setting – What will you notice is different if counselling begins to work for you?
Immediacy – You say you're not very good with words but you're very clear in the way you're explaining things to me.
Incompleted sentences – So that makes you want to ...

Indirect self-disclosure – Some people (drawing on your own experience professionally or personally) in similar situations find that it is helpful to … I wonder whether or not that would work for you.

Invitation to expand conversation – Would you like to say more about that?

Invitation to be specific and concrete – Could you give me a recent example of that?

Invitation to make contrasts – So is that what it was like last time or is it quite different?

Minimal prompts – mm, uh ha, yes, etc.

Normalizing – If you were to ask ten people passing on the street what they thought about what you were going through, what do you think they would say? If you were the counsellor, what would you be saying to a client who has just said what you've said? What do you think about other people who have got this problem?

Paraphrasing – When you're on your own your mind begins to turn to things which scare you.

Prioritizing/Focusing – From the various things you have said, I wonder which issue you would like to tackle first?

Questions (Open) – How will you know when things are getting better?

           (Closed) – How long have you been together now?

           (Circular)– So when you do that how will it affect your partner and will that make a difference to …?

Reflection/Mirroring – You're frightened.

Reframing – Tentative offer of an alternative view. 'Another way of looking at it might be that … '

Seeking clarification – I am not sure I understood you properly, could I just check that you were told at the hospital …

Summarizing – You have been trying very hard to overcome these feelings but until now nothing has worked for you.

Use of metaphors – The panic is a monster taking over your life.

Use of similes – So it is as if you are setting out on a long journey and you are not sure where it will end.

Box 1.3 *Solution-focused skills*

acknowledging and validating client
engaging in problem-free talk
exploring pre-session change
negotiating problem definition
goal setting
listening for strengths and exceptions
eliciting client competence and resources
facilitating client utilization
joining the client – matching language
using 'how' not 'why' questions

negotiating a reframe of the problem
amplifying change
seeking difference
normalizing
developing strategies
offering menus/multiple choice
both/and choices
miracle questions
relationship questions
scaling
giving client feedback
compliments
task giving
evaluating

THE SKILLS OF THE SOLUTION-FOCUSED COUNSELLOR

The interventions listed here will be described in Chapters 3, 4 and 5. The role of the counsellor is not to lead from the front but to follow the client. Although there are inescapable power dimensions to the role, the task of the counsellor is like that of the tugs which pull an ocean-going liner. It is the captain of the liner who charts its course and the liner which has the power to reach its destined port, yet the role of the tugs is to keep the liner on course, to get it started and to help it out of the harbour. It must point it in the right direction for the open sea. Not an insignificant role, especially if the sea and weather conditions are not favourable. The most obvious contrast between the skills used in the solution-focused approach and other forms of counselling is the centrality of questioning in the former. As with systemic therapy, the questions are the therapy.

Unconditional acceptance is in itself therapeutic for a client suffering from stress who feels he is struggling in a critical, hostile environment. Offering a relationship which validates and acknowledges the client's experience means the formation of the therapeutic alliance takes priority over diagnosis – which we know is not a reliable predictor of therapeutic outcome (Garfield and Bergin, 1994).

It may be due to its origins in strategic family counselling that scant attention has been paid in the solution-focused literature to the quality of the counsellor–client relationship. Feelings seemed to be ignored at the expense of observable behaviour; the outer life took precedence over the inner life. Empathy does not appear in the index of any of the key texts until 1996 (Miller *et al.*, 1996, 1997). O'Hanlon and Beadle (1994) described their approach as 'solution-oriented' (Possibility Therapy) to distinguish it from the perceived narrowness of the solution-focused label. They pay more attention to the quality of the therapeutic relationship than others. They use the terms 'acknowledge and validate' rather than 'empathy' but the meaning is the same. Recently authors have highlighted the importance of the core conditions of empathy, genuineness and unconditional positive regard and the need for counsellors to address fully the client's emotional concerns (Butler and Powers, 1996). Empathic rapport may emerge as clients sense the counsellor is genuinely working alongside them to meet their concerns. Empathy is demonstrated in the giving of support, encouragement and reinforcement.

Although in solution-focused counselling the ventilation of feelings is not considered to be a prerequisite for change, the important role emotions play in the change process is fully recognized. For example, if we suspend the common belief that clients must get in touch with their feelings and 'sort them out' in order for change to take place, we can open an alternative route which suggests that people can *raise their emotional awareness by experiencing themselves making changes.* Addressing emotions directly is not always productive. Hales (1999) argues that it is sometimes true if you feel painful feelings enough you come through to the other side but sometimes it is not.

> Sometimes the most helpful thing to do is to feel and experience the feeling as fully as possible, particularly with new feelings that are just coming into awareness. But sometimes the feeling is just that same old painful feeling again, going round and round, and feeling it one more time does not get the client any further. A solution-focused response would be to point out the choice and ask the client which would seem to them the most helpful thing to do. (p. 235)

Feelings change as we begin to live differently. As we begin to make changes our feelings change even more. For some clients directly addressing their feelings first will be the way for them to approach change. For others it may be through examining their thought processes or their current behaviour. Where clients are unsure about their problem, their feelings may be able to trace the source of their concern for them.

Although the solution-focused approach pays little attention to unconscious factors or to possible transference and counter-transference in the relationship, there is no reason why a solution-focused counsellor could not use her own inner feelings about the client in the 'here and now' to create a point of learning. This would be in addition to the feedback at the end of a session, when the counsellor will often share her feelings about the client. For example, she might say, 'I was really impressed when you managed to ...' or 'I was struck when you said that you had ... How did you do that?'. It goes without saying the counsellor must show due care and respect for the client's feelings. Failure to do so can result in the client sabotaging the counsellor's clumsy attempts to 'move things on'. Counsellors may explore feelings by questioning the client about them as they seek exceptions to the problem or as they develop answers to the miracle and scaling questions. When counsellors give feedback at the end of sessions highlighting what the client is doing well and what qualities they have demonstrated, clients are often emotionally moved. It may be the first time in their lives, or the first time in a long time, someone has publicly acknowledged the strengths and qualities which they have exhibited.

A holistic approach to the needs of clients, paying attention to the core values and conditions of counselling combined with an awareness of one's own values, helps to prevent the relationship from becoming a functional and mechanical one. This prevents a situation arising in which the counsellor deploys solution-focused formulae without heart or spirit. Being oneself is also important when there are temptations to follow charismatic gurus who appear to enjoy glittering success with all their clients.

Imitation may be the sincerest form of flattery but in a therapeutic relationship counsellors who are not being authentic are frequently caught out by their clients. Having watched many of the 'master practitioners' in action, it seems to me that they all counsel very differently. They even depart from their own textbooks as their own natural humour, wisdom, experience and personality come into play. Frank (1959) argued counsellors must project confidence in their chosen way of working but this confidence cannot be present if the counsellor is not at ease with the model being used. Communicating confidence creates trust in clients and can be a force for change. Whether counsellors choose their model or the model chooses them is a fascinating question. What is it about the counsellor which leads her or him to adopt a solution-focused approach? Given the optimistic, can-do feel about solution-focused work, does it attract people who have that approach to life? What are the main factors in the choice of a model – personal values/ training/supervision/colleagues/agency/ temperament/early childhood experiences? Nelson-Jones (2000) has argued the founders of therapy models, such as Rogers, Berne and Jung, all had experiences in their families of origin which profoundly affected their future work. As well as personal factors, prevailing cultural norms shape the rise and fall of therapies. The rise of brief therapy is surely not unconnected with a political climate which sits light on ideology and history and prefers a pragmatic approach.

From the client's point of view, opening yourself to someone who encourages you, who compliments and affirms you, who respects your individuality, who listens to you and who radiates hope and optimism is potentially a transforming experience. The solution-focused counsellor trusts the client's best instincts and treats him as a resourceful creative and imaginative person. In order to do this she must be optimistic, creative, imaginative and full of hope. The counsellor can slow down the change process by either (a) underestimating the client's capacity for change or (b) defining the problem in terms which make it insolvable. She may ignore or devalue the client's resources, even seeing them as part of the problem not as part of the solution. For example, a counsellor might consider a client's age to be a negative rather than a positive force.

The counsellor enhances rapport with the client by matching the client's language and use of imagery. Equally important is the discipline required to keep on 'a solution track' whilst allowing the client the space and time to articulate his concerns. Qualities such as patience, tenacity, warmth, tact and curiosity enable the counsellor to respectfully enter into the client's frame of reference. Since questioning is the principal intervention used, the counsellor needs to ensure it does not become an oppressive interrogation. To avoid this, the skilled counsellor will break the question –answer cycle by making empathic and reflective statements, offering minimal prompts and by sharing ideas with the client. The counsellor also needs to have good powers of concentration and the ability to recall and communicate back to clients vivid and accurate examples of their successes.

Being sensitive to the dynamics of the relationship will enable the counsellor to notice and respond appropriately to the stress signals conveyed by the client's body language. At times they will share reflective silences. Solution-focused counselling is not merely a set of techniques but a way of being 'present with' the client. It is a collaborative partnership in which the counsellor consults with the client to ensure they are working on what is important to the client. As Berg (1999: viii) states, 'We are most caring, loving and respectful of clients when we ask questions and listen to their ideas on how to improve their own lives, allowing them to decide what is best for them.' Freed from being an expert in the client's life yet owning counselling expertise and keeping boundaries, the counsellor can share her feelings, concerns and uncertainties in the helping role.

The counsellor needs considerable skill in moving with the client between problem-focused and solution-focused talk. If we think of it in terms of two islands (inspired by Bill O'Hanlon's Possibility/Problem Land) – one problem island and one solution island – clients are likely to feel more secure on problem island because it is familiar to them. They know the territory well, after all they have spent a lot of time there. They may take any number of helpers on tours of the island, pointing out places of particular interest and telling stories of what happened there at different times. There may even be some comfort for the guide in doing this. When the visitor invites the client to accompany them to solution island (by engaging in solution talk), the client may decline with thanks, citing all manner of reasons why it is not a good idea at this point in time. After some time the client may come to trust in the counsellor and decide with considerable ambivalence to go for a brief visit to solution island. But once they are there they usually soon feel the need to return to problem island ('there's no place like home'). Since both counsellor and client need to occupy the same therapeutic space, there is little point in the counsellor staying behind on solution island. For the client to spend more time on solution island he perhaps needs to experience that it is a good place and good things happen on it. In fact better things happen there than happen on problem island. For the counsellor's part she needs to be patient and understanding with the client's wish to keep a foot in both camps. The therapeutic alliance, the bond of trust, acceptance, understanding, respect and care becomes the bridge which allows free passage between the two islands. Some clients may of course accept the invitation to visit solution island more quickly than others. But when the invitation is declined, the counsellor needs to give the client more time and space to make choices. Clients and counsellors are fellow travellers who need to follow the same map if they are to reach their destination.

Clients under stress need different amounts of problem talk. For some people 'getting it off their chests' or 'dumping it on someone else' is highly therapeutic and may be all they need to soldier on. Being heard and believed for the first time by someone who does not judge them and is not shocked by their story or does not problem solve or give advice may be enough. The counsellor may only need to act as a witness as the client tells and rewrites his personal story. Most of the time solution-focused counsellors aim to act not so much as a skip as a recycling centre.

Even when clients are unable to move out of problem talk into solution talk the counsellor can ask coping questions which search for the client's resources. For example:

- How do you cope with all that happening to you?
- What helps you when things are difficult?
- Has it got worse or is this the worst it has ever been?
- Are you stronger now than you were last month/year?
- Which was the least bad day last week?
- Which was the best day?

- How does coming here help?
- On a scale of 0–10, with 0 being as bad as it's ever been, where would you say you were today?

The counsellor synchronizes her pacing and timing with the client. As they weave their narratives together, emotional and mental demands are made on both parties. Solution-focused counselling is not an easy alternative to medication or other forms of the 'talking cure', it can be difficult and tiring. For the counsellor, one of the biggest challenges is the need to work with much less information about the problem than most other counsellors would deem necessary. For people trained in other traditions this is initially anxiety provoking. Confidence in the process comes when they experience their clients changing, without them having engaged in their normal amount of information gathering. It is probably wise for new practitioners to incorporate solution-focused techniques into their practice gradually.

THE THERAPEUTIC RELATIONSHIP

These skills need to be used in the context of a therapeutic ethical relationship, otherwise the counsellor becomes a mere technician. Research consistently suggests that the human qualities communicated by the counsellor are what clients find most helpful, irrespective of whichever model is being used (Garfield and Bergin, 1994). These qualities include warmth, openness, genuineness, empathy and care. According to Mahoney and McRay Patteson (1992), the optimal therapeutic relationship should incorporate the following principles:

Be uniquely individual and respect diversity

The solution-focused emphasis on staying close to the client's goals and its refusal to develop counsellor-led hypotheses about problems ensures that each client explores solutions in a unique way. The counsellor always tries to work within the client's frame of reference.

Attend first to urgent issues

Whichever issue is a priority for the client is a priority for the counsellor. The counsellor works with what the client brings and does not believe that 'the real problem' lies elsewhere.

Offer a safe base for the client, one which is gently, patiently and consistently nurturing

The approach avoids confrontational interventions. It affirms the resources and competence of clients, even in the face of 'failure'. As with all therapies it can be done badly, in which case clients might feel unheard or pressurized to make progress of which they feel incapable.

Incorporate a rationale and meaningful rituals

The spirit of the model is to demystify therapeutic processes. It aims to give the skills and processes to clients, so that they can continue to use them for themselves. Prior to the start of counselling clients are introduced to the main beliefs and values of the approach. The roles of both parties will be discussed. There is a structure to the therapy which constructs rituals for beginnings and endings of each session.

Respect the client's unique perceptions and experiences

The emphasis is always on the counsellor joining the client, being a guest in his world, rather than the other way round. Solutions are sought which fit the person's unique profile, not the problem.

Model being human and mentally healthy

The approach allows counsellors to use their own personalities, humour and experience. Counsellors do not distance themselves by retreating behind an 'expert' role.

Work with the resistance of the client

The ambition is always to find ways of collaborating with clients, especially when the client does not trust the counsellor or is an involuntary client. As previously stated, resistance is reframed as a helpful communication from the client.

Seek to empower the client by respecting privacy and resilience

This may be accomplished by the counsellor assuming that the client has the qualities and skills required to solve the problem. The client cannot be seen as fragile but as strong and resilient. Empowerment is experienced in the sessions as the tone and tenor of the counsellor's questions imply that the client has the power and freedom to make choices.

The client's needs come first

This is a basic requirement of professional and ethical practice. Respect for the expressed needs (goals) of the client, the fostering of a collaborative partnership and giving the client credit for progress are some ways in which this takes place.

Prevention over corrective intervention

Solution-focused techniques do not belong to the counsellor, they are helpful only insofar as they can be taken away and used by clients on themselves. Once clients capture the spirit, the values and the techniques of the model, they are equipped to tackle future problems. Research conducted by the Brief Therapy Centre in Milwaukee suggests that this is indeed the case (De Jong and Hopwood, 1996).

RESEARCH ON SOLUTION-FOCUSED BRIEF THERAPY

The research on common factors in therapy and its relevance to the solution-focused model will be discussed in Chapter 6. We know from various studies that only approximately 15 per cent of the variance in client outcome is attributed to the specificity of the model being used (Lambert and Bergin, 1994).There are other apparently much more significant dimensions, such as extra-therapeutic factors, the therapeutic alliance, expectancy, hope and placebo factors. However, in a climate which demands evidence-based practice and promotes the use of treatment manuals, researchers are under pressure to demonstrate the efficacy of the model (product) being used. Much of solution-focused research to date has been conducted by research practitioners who are advocates for the model. More independent research is needed which adheres to protocols acceptable to the research community. A large number of studies are now being conducted throughout Europe and the United States.

There is a great deal of anecdotal evidence from practitioners who report the method is popular with clients, seems to accelerate change and has also enhanced their own job satisfaction. They suggest that solution-oriented conversations feel more affirming of their clients with the result that sessions generate more energy, hope and optimism. Some report surprising movement with clients who previously they considered to be hard going, stuck or resistant.

Gingerich and Eisengart (1999) reviewed fifteen controlled studies of solution-focused brief therapy in the literature. All of the studies which reported pre and post results indicated that clients had improved outcomes. In seven of the eleven studies which allowed comparison between the solution-focused approach and other standard treatments, the outcome from the former equalled or surpassed standard treatments. Sometimes it produced the same outcomes but in less time. According to Gingerich and Eisengart (1999: 3) much remains to be done to establish the research base for the therapy:

what is needed are more rigorously designed studies, studies using randomised designs, comparison groups of standard treatment; treatment manuals, monitoring of treatment integrity, multiple objective outcome measures, multiple vantage points of change (client, family/other, expert) and minimum one year follow up. In addition, replication is needed to verify that outcomes are generalisable across investigators and settings.

CHAPTER 2
A Solution-Focused Model of Stress

A theory of therapy outlines the parameters for what is to be included or excluded from the therapeutic process. It offers a script for the counsellor and client to follow. It promotes a particular kind of relationship and advocates specific forms of discourse for the client to use in the reworking of her problem narrative. As noted in the previous chapter, the solution-focused approach emerged from close and lengthy observations of clinical practice by de Shazer, Berg and their colleagues. This commitment to be 'practice led' still characterizes the research and theoretical development of the model. As the number of solution-focused practitioners in different countries grows and their work with different client groups is reported in the literature, the practical and theoretical base of the model is strengthened.

The theory underpinning the solution-focused model is not a theory about problems or the people who have them. It is a theory or a description of what happens in therapy (Korman, 1997). The irony is despite the fact that solution-focused techniques are simple to understand the concepts behind them are complex. The theoretical background includes the following elements which I shall explore in turn, with particular reference to stress counselling:

- a social constructionist view of reality
- therapy as narrative
- a view about causality of events
- the image of the person as a social being
- change as a central focus.

A SOCIAL CONSTRUCTIONIST VIEW OF REALITY

Solution-Focused Therapy belongs to a school of therapies which have emerged over the past 40 years and which can be described broadly as constructionist or social constructionist. These include, among others, the Personal Construct approach (Kelly, 1955), Neuro-Linguistic Programming (Bandler and Grinder, 1979), the

Mental Research Institute (MRI) Brief Problem Solving Model (Watzlawick *et al.*, 1974) and the Narrative approach (White and Epston, 1990). There are many differences between these models (and their main proponents can be territorial about them) but they share a set of ideas which set them apart from other therapeutic traditions.

These ideas come from the emerging school of Social Constructionism. Among the main writers about a Social Constructionist approach to psychotherapy are Gergen (1999) and McNamee (1992). Social constructionism is a post-modern philosophy. It takes as its starting point that reality is socially negotiated. There is no fixed, stable, objective reality which can be discovered. Reality is 'invented' (Watzlawick, 1984) in meaning-making between people. Piaget (1954) described the dynamic interactive processes of knowing as assimilation and accommodation. We adapt to and are changed by new knowledge, which is itself shaped by our existing constructs as they attempt to assimilate the information. Having assimilated new information we then accommodate it through newly organized schema or schemata (the building blocks of knowledge).

There is no detached body of knowledge separate from the human construction of it. Since there is no objective attainable truth, there are multiple ways in which people assimilate and accommodate it to their experiences. How people construct their world is imbedded in language. Language is contextualized and relative to a particular time, place, individual or group (Berg and De Jong, 1996). People attempt to make sense of their experience by negotiating with others. In the case of counselling this takes the form of a specific type of conversation which follows its own rules. From a social constructionist point of view, stress is not an objective condition or illness which people have. This would be to reify it. It is a language construct negotiated in a specific social context to describe a range of meanings people attach to feelings, thoughts and behaviours. When people cannot cope with a particular level of stress they reach the outer limits of their social construction of their place in the world. Their constructions in relation to their abilities are challenged. Their constructions about other people, their reliability, competence and opinions are undermined and need to be renegotiated. Their constructions about their place in the world are likewise shaken, as is their sense of safety, value and purpose. As a result the world is constructed as hostile, threatening, uncaring and ruthless. If the crisis is sudden, people will have been unable to adjust their ideas, their expectations and their behaviour. Their cognitive abilities will not have adapted yet to this new knowledge or experience. It will feel as if this experience has undermined or even sabotaged constructions. By this I mean values, perceptions, memories and predictions built over a long period of time. These personal constructions will have developed their validity and power not in isolation but in the person's community or social groups.

As I write this chapter, the company which produces cars in the city in which I live is threatening to close its plant. For decades producing cars has been an integral part of the collective and personal identity of the city and many of its citizens. Many of them can remember with pride previous generations of their family who worked for the company. The closure of the plant would rob people not only of their present and future but also of their memories. The threat to people's livelihood is already producing high levels of personal and communal stress. If the plant were to close, the workers and their families would need to radically change how they construct their personal and social worlds. Many other people who depend upon the plant for their livelihood would also need to make major adaptations to their lives. This feels like a powerful threat to the whole community. If the community can come together to express a collective meaning for the crisis it is easier for individuals to cope with their level of stress. Communities with strong social bonds and shared values have a sense of solidarity which sustains them. Fragmented communities in which individuals are isolated struggle to deal with this level of communal and personal stress. To cope with the stress communities find ways to communicate the meaning of these events in their lives. This is done through meetings, demonstrations, informal support and the use of the media. How the individual copes depends not only upon the community's ability to construct a response but also on that person's past constructions in relation to loss, threat and crisis. People need to build their resources and strengths to meet the demands of the situation. In other words they need to adapt and survive.

People construct and share language according to the audience for whom their performances or stories are intended. We borrow the language of medicine to negotiate our perceived illness or pain with the doctor. We adopt a different language to describe our illness to our partner, possibly with the purpose of gaining social approval for the sick role. We use the language of social courtesy when talking to a work colleague about our illness. If we confuse these languages, using them in the wrong context for the wrong audience, there is an absence of social fit. It is from our culture that we learn and invent the language to communicate and generate new words to fit social experiences. The use of the term 'stress' in a psychological context is of fairly recent origin, but it has become so overused it has lost its value.

In order to work with clients who describe their problem as due to stress, a constructionist approach will:

- Give precedence to the client's perceptions and experiences, rather than to 'the facts' (which are unattainable). In a sense the client does not have a problem when she comes for help, she brings an issue for negotiation. It is in the conversation between the counsellor and the client that the 'reality' of the client is formed. Meaning is socially negotiated in the solution-focused approach by a counsellor-led conversation the rules of which allow interventions such as exception seeking and the miracle question. At the same time the rules exclude other interventions which are designed for different purposes in other therapies, for example, making interpretations of the client's material.
- Use the multiplicity of narratives which clients could choose to bring about the changes they want. Part of the clients' problems may be the limited range of perspectives she brings to the situation. Her current stories about herself are proving self-defeating and problem-making. She needs a new and equally real/ true narrative which will give her options for the future. For the social constructionist counsellor the 'right' narrative is one which works for the client in her social context. Different clients will need different narratives. A key task for the counsellor is to seek difference. This means challenging the ways language creates or hides different stories with different meanings. Where there are other stories to be told there are other roles/qualities/resources to claim. Where there are differences in explaining how problems happen there are new possibilities for solving them.

- Emphasize the importance of joining with the client in order to co-create a new and empowering narrative. The counsellor does not occupy a superior or privileged position from which to reshape the client's story. Instead the counsellor respects the client's frame of reference and seeks to meet them where they are.
- Invite the counsellor to affirm the expertise and unique experience of the client and to disown a privileged position of knowledge and power. A non-expert stance is taken.
- Pay attention to the context in which the client's narrative developed. One implication of this is that all problems are seen as social as well as personal. It is not possible to have a totally individualized problem. Problems are negotiated within a community of people.
- Acknowledge competence and strengths. This intervention invites the client to shift their own reading of the situation and begin to see it in a different light. One which is more balanced, hopeful and affirming.
- Ensure that the counsellor develops a clear sense of his or her own values, blind-spots and biases (O'Connell, 1998). The solution-focused literature is silent about the need for counsellors to receive personal therapy or engage in personal development. But given the highly influential role of the counsellor it is essential that the counsellor knows the context of his or her own knowledge and experience.
- Encourage reflexivity by the client (Berg and De Jong, 1996). All therapies provide space for clients to take stock and review their situation from observational positions which they have not taken previously. The solution-focused frame or filter, through which clients reflect upon their problems, is future-oriented, change/solution-focused and resource-aware. It offers a different frame to that which is offered by problem-focused therapies.

THERAPY AND NARRATIVE

In a court of law the defence and the prosecution set out to establish the facts – the truth of the matter. They are committed to finding historical truth, i.e. what actually happened on the night in question. However, in therapy the quest for truth takes a different form. Because the client comes with a story, she comes with a reconstructed version of events. She presents her story in a particular way for a particular audience. The counsellor is not in a position to find out what 'really' happened. He does not have access to that kind of knowledge. He therefore concerns himself with the client's personal truth, her perception and memories. In working with this subjectivity the counsellor helps the client to make sense of her experiences. If the client reports how stressed she is in her personal relationships the counsellor does not and cannot establish the accuracy of her reports. Having her partner join the conversation will add a new dimension to the original story. It may throw new light upon it but it will not confer objectivity upon it. Each story-teller has a vested interest and a particular position from which he or she views the situation. Since there are many stories the client could choose to tell and indeed many different versions of the same one, the one(s) which facilitate change for the client are those which are most appropriate in this context.

The narrative approach of writers such as White and Epston (1990) attends to the ways in which people present themselves to the world in the stories they tell about themselves and which others tell about them. People's lives are shaped by these stories. In a globalized and multicultural society there are many identity stories which a person can adopt. The Internet gives people the opportunity to assume virtual identities which are unverifiable. Identities may be eclectic. People may choose, for example, to come out as gay in one particular grouping but retain their privacy in less tolerant environments. The strain of maintaining dual identities can, however, be a major source of stress.

In reality there are limitations on the stock of stories which people can adopt about themselves. One cannot become exactly whom one wants. There are structures which limit people and reduce opportunities. There are glass ceilings, quotas and barriers which ensure how far some groups of people are allowed to advance. These discriminatory social narratives may have evolved over a long period of time to such an extent that those who support them are not even aware of them. Institutional racism or sexism need not be immediately evident but can permeate the culture in myriad ways. When counsellors explore personal narratives of clients it is important to remember they are imbedded in a social, economic and political context.

On the individual level, when people relate stories about themselves, they edit their material for their audience. In therapy where clients tend not to know the conversational rules, they will be guided in their story-telling by the counsellor's overt or covert rules for social discourse. The counsellor cannot avoid influencing the client as they construct together certain kinds of stories. The very act of giving time and space to clients influences the shape of their stories.

EXAMPLE

One of Martin's key stories about himself is that as a result of two failed marriages he considers himself to be a failure at personal relationships. This story is an identity story which has changed over the years as he has told and retold it to different people. When he told it to people who were themselves divorced their response was very different from those who were in either stable and happy relationships or those for whom an exclusive long-term relationship was not a priority. Audience participation in his story affected his telling and retelling of it. It changed the way he eventually integrated his story into other stories about his life. When he retold the story in different contexts it was shaped by that context. It would have taken on a different meaning when he spoke with someone:

- struggling with a commitment issue
- recovering from a broken relationship
- trying to effect a reconciliation in a relationship
- coping with a conflict between work and a relationship.

McLeod (1997) writes about two processes which take place as the counsellor works with the client's stories. First, there is differentiation in which rival narratives, different but equally plausible stories told about the same events, must be generated ... The client who previously could tell only one 'problem story' finds with the assistance of the therapist that he or she has available alternative accounts of his or her troubles. (p. 70)

The second process is one of integration where one of the competing narratives emerges as (a) more coherent, more accurate and or widely applicable and (b) able to subsume the subordinate narrative. For this integration to be owned by the client it is essential that the rewrite be not too far removed from the original, otherwise the client will not agree to the fit. This can be a danger in an over-optimistic, solution-focused rewrite. If the new story is too positive too soon the client will not recognize him or herself and will disown it by resisting the counsellor's retelling. A solution-focused rewrite will incorporate elements missing from the problem-dominated story. By this I mean what the client considered to be of marginal importance. This expanded story will do more justice to the person because it encompasses neglected or undervalued 'truths' about him. It will place a different slant on how the problem is framed. It will build into the story values, beliefs, attitudes, choices, strategies and feelings which give the person a new and more balanced identity. The client will be able to say, 'I am not a problem, I can use a lot of what is right with me'. The story can also furnish a new reading of the social context to which it belongs, one with possibilities but also with oppressive structures. These new narratives aim to empower the client 'to create stories they can live by and live with' (McLeod, 1997: 86). In one of de Shazer's videos of his work (1998) he explores two parallel stories with a client who is a young drug user. One story she tells about herself is described by her as 'The Right Path' and the other as 'The Other Path'. De Shazer skilfully allows her to further explore both paths and choose for herself which story she wants to live by. This new narrative is a progressive one in which 'events are lined in such a way that one steadily progresses toward a goal' (Gergen and Gergen, 1986: 27).

CAUSALITY

Conventional therapy seeks to provide the client with a rationale for her problems and an understanding of their origins. Most forms of structural therapy assume there is a truth out there that is discoverable. This 'truth' lies underneath the surface – the ubiquitous iceberg. The therapists approach the client's problems from an efficient causality angle, i.e. what has produced this effect in the client's life? The role of the counsellor is to gather information about the client's problems and help her to track down what may have caused and may still be causing her problems. There can be no certainty in this quest, at best it is informed guesswork. In any given situation there could be multiple ways of accessing the causes of the client's problems. If we take as an example a person who suffers from stress at work, the client's inability to cope could be linked to a range of issues at various levels and which have historical, current and future dimensions.

Possible causes for stress

culture of workplace
job insecurity
political and economic policies
lack of time management skills
promotion beyond competence
underemployment/frustration
lack of support from managers
unworkable systems
lack of resources
poor working conditions (for example, noise, space, light and heating)
discrimination in terms of pay and opportunities
health problems
lack of prospects, flexible working hours, maternity leave
life/work imbalance
poor relationship with partner
child care conflicts
travel stress
conflict with colleague(s)
lack of control over workload
lack of variety in workload
lack of autonomy in decision-making
lack of role models
family upbringing – values, scripts, traumas, learning
personality, e.g. super conscientious
previous history of stressful situations
influence of peers/friends.

There is a complex interaction between the working environment and the client's personal history, resources and current circumstances. What should the focus of the work be? And in what proportions? How does the counsellor know how to attribute causality? To focus on the client herself may be to pathologize a healthy individual when it is the working situation itself which is sick. To blame the system would be to ignore the unique ways in which the individual participates in that system.

The counsellor would also have a choice whether to explore the here and now which may be close to the client's agenda or the past where inferences become more speculative. Making links with past events, especially early childhood experiences, may not fit the client. There could be a mismatch between the language system the counsellor uses and the client's frame of reference. In deference to the expert position of the counsellor the client may accept his formulation of the problem but not own it. The formulation may in some cases oppress the client into thinking her situation is predetermined and unchangeable. As a result of the counsellor's hypothesis the client may terminate counselling. In some cases this might be construed by the counsellor or the agency as resistance and the client's departure as failure. Even where this is not the outcome and where the client accepts the counsellor's hypothesis as proposed in the language and rules of the counsellor's therapy model, there is still the next step of bridging the explanation with strategies for the future. Even well-constructed explanations may not shed light on what the client needs to do to make progress. Some explanations actually close down or deter the client from making changes. Some attribute blame, as distinct from appropriate accountability. Some lock the client into passivity whilst some invalidate the client's experiences (O'Hanlon and Beadle, 1994). Some theories of therapy trace the origins of problems back not to personal choice but to deterministic intrapsychic or environmental forces. This unsought inheritance programmes the degree of choice and power the client has to change the course of her life.

Since the solution-focused counsellor does not pursue the search for causes and origins but suspends belief about them, an enormous burden is lifted off his shoulders. This opens therapeutic space for the counsellor to use in a different way. Instead of looking for the history of the client's stopping places to date, the solution-focused counsellor helps her to find out how she could reach her preferred destination. It approaches causality from the other end, final causality. The present is shaped by the past but it is also influenced by the future. What we do today is because of what we want to happen tomorrow. Studying for exams when the sun is shining outside is tolerable only on account of the long-term benefit which will come from passing them. Our future goals shape our present. A person's sense of her future may be a lot clearer and more accessible than her memories of the past, although this may not be the case for someone who is depressed and unable to visualize the future. If you know what you want to happen or at least know the next step forward, even if you do not have a long-term vision, this is more likely to lead to immediate focused change than an explanation which may or may not throw light on what to do next. This preference for working backwards from the future is one of the elements in the model which makes solution-focused counselling brief. It does not take as much time to work out the future as it does to make sense of the past.

IMAGE OF THE PERSON

The image of the human person in the Social Constructionist approach is that of the person as a social agent. To understand the person she or he needs to be seen in a cultural context, i.e. in a human community and in relationships. Meaning and purpose in living come from the meaning-making community. In traditional societies there used to be a unitary consensus about the meaning of actions and the role that individuals held within the community. Such a community shared the same view about the world through their beliefs, values and traditions. Their socially constructed world bound them together in strong and enduring social networks.

In contemporary western societies, however, this social glue has come unstuck. There are many competing world views which attract the support of sections of the community. There is a fragmentation of opinions and convictions. The dominant world view, which has ruled and controlled the community and the individuals within it, has been undermined. The social networks have been weakened or downgraded and alternative meaning structures have been created. These may be based around work or friendship or common interest. They need not be geographically close. The loosening of the social fabric now allows individuals to adopt ways of living, social identities and belief systems less dependent upon authority and social control. They are likely to be multiple and diverse. As a result of the cultural shift away from conformity there are fewer community sanctions and limitations on personal choice and freedom. Individuals have to learn to tolerate lifestyles different from their own.

In western society where the autonomy of the individual is prized this widening of choice in all areas of life brings both threat and insecurity, as well as opportunity and gain. Without the clear signposts, rules, norms and standards of a stable society, the individual has to take responsibility for her choices. This is often without role models or precedents to help. This makes for stressful decision-making. It can be acutely painful and stressful for those caught between cultures, those who are trying to construct an identity which fits contemporary society, yet does not exclude them from their own communities and traditions. In many cultures, counselling values, such as the autonomy of the individual, self-actualization and personal choice, are quite foreign. They conflict with the primacy of the community over the individual.

Stress arises from a gap between how people experience themselves and how they would like to be perceived by others – a conflict between their 'ordinary' self and their 'idealized' self. This tense dichotomy may generate feelings of shame, guilt, anxiety, regret and self-blame. A reappraisal of our personal history might help us to bring these two 'selfs' closer together. As Butler and Powers (1996) state, 'we need to know our history or we risk never being able to repeat the successes of the past' (p. 229).

Social constructionism leads counsellors to explore not what is *within* (intrapsychic) people, as if there was an inner world divorced from a cultural, anthropological context, but to examine what lies *between* people, i.e. an interactional perspective. Feelings, thoughts and actions take place within the linguistic negotiations in which people engage. Meanings are always open for renegotiation. As McLeod (1997) states, 'The notion of the "external" signifies a move away from an image of the person as somehow possessing an autonomous, inner self requiring continual exploration and attention toward a sense of persons as engaged in action, immersed in a culture, as storied and story-making beings' (p. 89). In solution-focused work when the client uses 'inner world' language the counsellor normally invites her to explore the meaning of those feelings in terms of 'outer world' relationships.

EXAMPLE

Client:	I feel really cold and sad inside.
Counsellor:	What happens to you when you feel like that?
Client:	I withdraw from those around me. I keep myself to myself.
Counsellor:	How do other people respond to that?
Client:	My partner gets really fed up with me. She thinks I should talk to her about it.
Counsellor:	If you did, what difference would that make to her?
Client:	She said she could help me more if I talked to her. If I included her in what I was doing.
Counsellor:	What might she do to help you if she felt you were including her more?
Client:	She would probably put her arms around me and tell me to stop worrying so much.
Counsellor:	How would that be helpful for you?
Client:	I would not feel so much on my own I suppose.

The inner experience of the client is placed in a relationship context. It is then explored in terms of the sequence of events which results from a shift in perceptions. Very different conversations emerge depending upon the type of language employed in negotiating the problem.

CHANGE

The client's experience of stress is in a constant state of change. It varies almost from minute to minute and certainly from hour to hour. For the solution-focused counsellor, it is this constantly evolving picture which is the focus of enquiry and action. She is change/solution-focused, as contrasted with counsellors who see the purpose of therapy as treatment/cure or personal development/growth.

The aim of solution-focused counselling is to help people to make changes in their situation. These changes should be enduring, not just superficial or temporary, although even temporary respite from one's problems can be therapeutic. Solution-focused counselling is not a quick fix which leaves fundamental problems untouched to surface again in another guise, at another time. To be more accurate, the aim is to help people become aware of the processes of change which have already begun and to find ways of continuing or amplifying them. These changes may take place at different levels depending upon the needs of the clients. They are holistic and systemic in their impact. It is not the role of the counsellor to argue the case for change. In fact counsellors may adopt a sceptical or quizzical view about the changes the client wants in order to make the client argue for change. This may take the form of questions such as:

- Who sees this as a problem?
- What is the incentive for making these changes?
- What would you be giving up?
- What problems might change bring about?
- Is there anything about the present situation you want to make sure you do not lose if you make changes?

Not all therapeutic approaches are interested in how people change:

> Whether theorising about systemic homeostasis, the equilibrium maintaining dynamics of ego defences, or reinforcement contingencies, most models focus on how clients are the same rather than how they are different, better, or improved from week to week.
> (Miller *et al.*, 1997: 41)

The counsellor's interest in the changes the client wants is reflected in the range of questions which focus on this theme. What would you like to change? How would that change be helpful for you? How did you manage to make that change? Would you like more or less of that in your life? How long do you think it will be before things start to change? What will you notice first? For some clients questions about change come as a welcome relief from questions about problems. It is perhaps unsurprising the client should be eager to engage in change talk. For it is the desire for change which has brought them into counselling, even if they feel ambivalent about it. Inevitably change brings gains and losses and poses complex dilemmas:

- How much do you want this?
- How much are you willing to pay emotionally/psychologically/socially for it?

While exploring what change has to offer them clients first need to acknowledge they have the power to make choices. They do not have to be slaves to the 'shoulds, oughts and musts' they inherited. People suffering from stress will often be living out heavy scripts they were given and which drive them into situations not of their own choosing and with which they cannot cope. Counselling can reveal these hidden drivers and open up possibilities for rewriting the script. In the case of stress counselling, this rewrite might not be about raising one's threshold of stress but of lowering it so that it can be prevented rather than coped with (Carlson, 1997).

In examining the ebb and flow of change, the counsellor paces his questions in order to open therapeutic space and to offer the client new or different ways of thinking about situations. The counsellor is curious about what is already happening or could happen in the client's life. The client is recruited into using change-oriented language. Depending upon the willingness and ability of the client to engage in this way, the counsellor either continues to develop the theme of change or allows the client to give a further account of the problem. Typical questions used at this stage include:

- What have you come here today to change?
- What is happening at the moment which makes you more hopeful that you can change the situation?
- What is different about your situation now that made you decide it was time to come for help and try to sort things out?

As people make changes in their behaviour, they can begin to change their understanding of how and why they acquired their problems in the first place. As they see things differently, they can begin to make further changes and to continue to deepen their understanding. It is a false dichotomy to split the process of self-understanding from the real world in which people experience themselves and search for meaning in their lives. It is of course possible to 'have the experience and miss the meaning'. In a highly stressed society in which people have little time to stop, activism can become a substitute for serious critical reflection. There are a lot of stressed people on the run who have forgotten what it is that they are trying to escape from!

Figure 2.1 outlines a solution-focused model of stress. The model illustrates the following points:

- the socially constructed nature of stress
- the perception of the client that an event represents a threat to resources which they consider to be important
- the need to challenge the negative, problem-ridden narrative which disempowers the person

Figure 2.1 *Solution-focused model of stress*

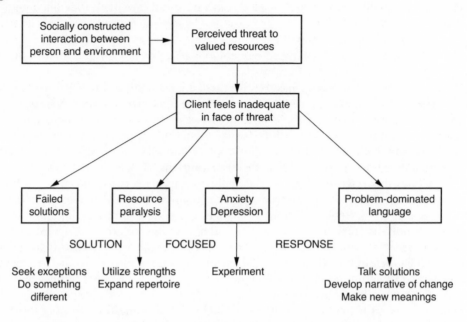

- the loss of a sense of competence and control when under stress
- the temporary destabilization or paralysis of the client's normal coping mechanisms
- the temporary eclipse of the person's strengths, qualities and personal resources
- the recovery of these by paying attention to exceptions to the problem
- the expansion of the client's skill repertoire.

ASSUMPTIONS

The solution-focused approach to stress makes a number of assumptions:

- People are basically competent and deal with pressures in living but at times they experience difficulties which they mostly overcome themselves with the help of friends, family and the community.
- Stress is a normal part of life. Having problems is normal. Life is full of problems. Once you solve one problem another one comes along. For some clients, knowing that what they are experiencing is normal, appropriate and healthy in the circumstances is in itself therapeutic. They were afraid that they were going mad. An accumulation of problems can overstretch an individual's normal coping capacity. Experiencing difficulties does not mean that the person is sick (and therefore in need of a cure) or damaged and in need of repair.
- People are resilient, creative problem-solvers but they often fail to pay sufficient attention to their 'non-problem' times. For example, times when they are using their resources to manage the problem.

- Problems happen in the interaction between the person and his or her social environment. They do not belong to the person as if he or she lived in a vacuum. People have experiences which are described as problematic by themselves and others but people themselves are not problems. There is always much more to a person than the problem. Discarding a problem identity, as a victim, for example, may be a step on the road to recovery.
- Small change can build an impetus for further change. This is achieved by breaking the process of change into small manageable steps. According to Rosenbaum, *et al.* (1990) there are three advantages to this:
  (1) It takes the pressure off both counsellor and client so that neither tries too hard;
  (2) The client is more likely to be willing and able to make a small change than a big one;
  (3) Any kind of movement may suffice to ignite hope in the client.

Generating hope and confidence is an important ingredient in brief counselling. The solution-focused way is to help the client make a small but significant step forward. Experiencing progress can restore the person's sense of agency and encourage the making of further changes. The recognition of small improvements by redressing a preoccupation with failure and pathology can encourage both the client and the counsellor. If small changes are celebrated a new ecology of success can start and new narratives about the clients can be written. The effect could be compared to a kaleidoscope in which the slightest rearrangement of the pieces produces a quite different picture. Looking out for small changes and giving clients feedback whenever change is discovered and spreading 'news of difference' to other significant people can raise the expectations of everyone in the client's social network. It can turn the observers into witnesses for change. It creates a feedback loop of success, a new culture in which what is right takes pre-eminence over what is wrong. This feedback becomes mutually reinforcing and forms the basis for a positive self-fulfilling prophecy. To some extent people live up to or down to the expectations and reinforcing behaviour of those around them. For Erickson (Zeig and Munion, 1999) the therapeutic process had a 'snowballing effect' whereby resources could be mobilized to address not only the original problem but other problems in the client's life. This optimistic sense of forward movement stands in contrast to the pessimistic notion that the elimination of a client's symptoms means that it will reappear elsewhere in the client's life.

If the client experiences change early in the counselling the client feels the process is credible. It encourages and sustains clients who expected it would take a long time before they experienced improvement.

- Take one small step at a time. 'It's not the size of the mountain ahead of you that stops your climbing it, but the grain of sand in your shoe.' Stress often brings a sense of powerlessness and loss of control. The client may feel overwhelmed and defeated before she starts. As a consequence she may deny the reality of the problem or seek ways of escaping from it. To reduce the size of the challenge it helps to break the problem-solving process into small steps with small attainable goals. It helps to take one day at a time. This avoids the frustration which follows the failure to attain over-ambitious goals.

The principles and practices of Milton Erickson (1901–80), a unique and charismatic psychotherapist, have been highly influential in the development of Brief Therapy. According to Zeig and Munion (1999), the former of whom is the Founder and Director of The Milton H. Erickson Foundation in Phoenix, Arizona, six core principles informed Erickson's work:

1. Problems are non-pathological and result from people trying to adapt to troublesome situations.
2. In most cases the person has adequate resources, strengths and experiences to resolve the problem.
3. In order to be effective the counsellor must use everything the client uniquely brings to therapy.
4. The counsellor may be active and directive.
5. The unconscious mind is an important tool in directing the therapeutic process.
6. Permanent change comes from the client experimenting in making changes outside of the sessions. (p. 26)

As we explore the process of Solution-Focused Brief Therapy, we shall see how most of these principles are imbedded in the model. Something of the spirit of Erickson's work also continues in the solution-focused emphasis on humour, spontaneity and creativity.

PROCESS OF SOLUTION-FOCUSED BRIEF THERAPY

Solutions not problems

Some people find the term 'solution' unhelpful and off-putting. It seems to imply that there is a solution for all of life's problems, when obviously this is not the case. An alternative title might be Change-focused Therapy or Future-oriented Therapy (O'Connell, 1998). A radical feature of the model is that it divorces the solution–construction process from the 'problem' itself. It takes the view there is no intrinsic connection between the problem and the solutions the client will generate to meet his goals. In a sense, it does not matter what the client presents as his problem, the solution-focused counsellor will adopt a similar stance towards it:

* to acknowledge the client's concerns
* to develop ways of framing the problem which will make change more possible, more quickly
* to seek exceptions to the problem
* to ask questions about the future
* to explore the client's strengths, qualities and previous solutions
* to help the client find small steps forward
* to compliment the client on what they are doing right.

The counsellor engages with the person primarily and only secondarily with the problem. Problem exploration takes place according to the degree demanded by the client. Solution-focused stress counselling does not significantly depart from the structure used with clients who bring other problems. An awareness of the dynamics of stress and theories about its causation can, however, be helpful for the counsellor. Many clients will be unable to engage in solution-oriented talk without a basic understanding of the mechanics of stress. An informed counsellor will be able to provide this information and be able to ask pertinent questions. An informed counsellor will be familiar with the raft of strategies available for overcoming stress and where appropriate will make these available to the client.

One down position

A 'one down' position is favoured by the solution-focused counsellor. This means that the counsellor relinquishes the role of expert, with its assumption that the counsellor has access to knowledge which the client does not have. It also means that the counsellor genuinely learns from the client how to be helpful to him. This is done by entering deeply into the client's perspective; being curious about what works for him; showing respect for his resourcefulness and by refusing to lead him overtly or covertly towards solutions preferred by the counsellor. The counsellor joins with the clients, matches his language and cooperates with his unique ways of dealing with his difficulties.

Resource awareness

Appropriate pressure which typically stimulates and aids optimum performance becomes a stressor when a person cannot summon the resources to cope. The person may lack the appropriate skills or not know how to apply them. They may have compounded the difficulty by responding to the pressure in ways which have themselves become part of the problem, e.g. working even harder or drinking more.

Clients may have problems because they are not aware of their resources. They may have defined their problem in ways which make it less solvable or they may be using a limited repertoire of skills or have adopted faulty strategies (failed solutions).

Hobfoll (1998) speaks about the things people value as 'resources'. He defined resources as

> the objects, conditions, personal characteristics, and energies that are either
> themselves valued for survival, directly or indirectly, or that serve as a means of
> achieving these resources. (p. 45)

What constitutes resources for any person or group of people is culturally conditioned. Resources are valued insofar as they meet the demands of a specific environment. They are needed to ensure the survival of the individual or the group in the face of an external threat. From this socio-cultural perspective Hobfoll identifies the key characteristic of stress:

Stress is predicted to occur as a result of circumstances that represent a threat of resource loss, or (2) actual loss of the resources required to sustain the individual-nested-in, family-nested-in social organisation.

In addition, because people will invest in what they value to gain further, stress is predicted to occur (3) when individuals do not receive reasonable gain for themselves or social group following resource investment, this itself being an instance of loss. (p. 46)

The perceived threat to the resources of the individual or the group is socially constructed in the interaction between the demands of the environment, mediated through people, and the individual's reading of those demands in relation to his assessment of resources available. From this viewpoint stress is neither a property of the environment, nor a deficit in the individual. It is a dynamic process between the two. Stress is imbedded in overlapping contexts. By this I mean the range of social organizations, such as work, home and community, in which the meaning of what is happening is linguistically shaped and given a name. There is no objective state or condition which can be discovered and labelled as 'stress'.

The constructionist view is that there are multiple ways of describing a situation. Some of these will contradict or exclude others and some will sit more easily alongside others. What one person will describe as stress may be seen by others as excitement and challenge. Similarly, what one person will define as an unreasonable work overload will be seen by others as manageable targets. The meaning attached to the reading of the situation depends upon the power base and vested interest of the person commenting. Whoever is employing the term 'stress' is actively creating a meaning for it. That meaning is a 'meaning for a purpose'. Words are doing 'things'. Consequences flow from the acceptance of the 'reality' which is created by the language. To retain a powerful position it is of crucial importance to control the language used in order to dictate the meaning and purpose of words. Politicians and propagandists have always known this. In more recent times the media and the advertising industry, in particular, have become word-crafters who know how to generate powerful images. They use language which connects with and resonates for consumers. If the target groups absorb and retain the advertiser's language and the realities it creates – often ones in which people are successful, attractive, loved or respected – then they become customers for the products which promise such an attractive life. When the dominant power in society has a monopoly of linguistic usage it can determine exactly what words will mean to people. Minority or dissenting voices are repressed or marginalized. The control of language in the western world still lies principally with a white, male elite. For example, legislation fails to reflect the day-to-day experiences of stress minority groups suffer. If their reality was given legitimacy in the public sphere, there would be stronger and more effective enforcement of anti-discriminatory legislation. It could be argued that the dominant discourse about stress is led by the middle class and as a result we hear less about the stress produced by bad housing, poverty, unemployment and poor public services. We need to adopt a critical stance to the linguistic context of stress. What is deemed to be stress in a white person may be construed as mental illness in a black person (Atkinson, 1985). Someone with a middle-class background may be diagnosed as suffering from ME whereas someone from a socially deprived area might be labelled lazy and workshy. Stress may be linguistically in vogue for people under pressure at work but not for a carer at home trying to cope with small children or an elderly relative. These people are more likely to describe themselves, and to be diagnosed, as depressed rather than stressed and be offered medication rather than counselling.

This tension is highlighted in the narrative negotiations which characterize the counselling conversation. These conversations are meaning-making exercises conducted according to the rules of therapeutic discourse. These include power differentials, privileged expertise, role boundaries and process structures. How wide is the range of languages available to counsellor and client to negotiate this meaning? Are there specific languages which are more helpful than others? The aim of solution-focused counselling is to raise the client's awareness of their own solutions and resources and to help them to expand their repertoire. Successfully tapping into available resources will narrow the gap between the perceived threat and the person's ability to handle it. This is particularly true if the client can channel and focus resources in a planned and effective way. The resources include the client's cultural strengths, values and traditions. Counsellors need to acknowledge access to these personal and social resources is limited, not only by the individual herself but also by the structures which shape the client's context. In addition, at times of serious stress people may be unable to activate their own resources as they would in normal times. Stress can be debilitating. It can blunt the person's sense of judgement. Negative thinking can then misread the situation in ways which maximize the scale of the threat and minimize awareness of the resources to contend with it.

The counsellor facilitates the client's awareness of resources by helping her to:

- identify and own the exceptions to the problems
- discover their own competence, qualities and strengths
- recall past solutions and transferable skills
- recognize what is within their control
- clarify and visualize the future
- identify the knowledge and skills needed to make a difference
- understand how the future, as well as the past, shapes the present.

As an integral part of this learning, clients become aware of how they edit and process the information they receive. They begin to identify the prisms through which they develop a perspective on life. In some cases, this can reveal self-limiting and self-defeating attitudes which had a part in creating the problem in the first place or are sustaining it in the present. Change may need to take place at the 'level' of these fundamental beliefs. This reappraisal will be necessary for some clients but not for others. Some clients unable to tap into their own resources at the start of counselling may be able to at a later stage, perhaps after they have been helped to acquire relaxation or positive imagery skills (Milner and Palmer, 1998).

Problem definition

How clients initially define or describe their problem(s) depends upon the language at their disposal. They may have borrowed terms and concepts from any number of sources, for example, peers, family, professionals and the media. Stress is the contemporary term for a whole host of difficult emotional, psychological, physiological and behavioural experiences. It is a sufficiently vague term to be used for almost any psychological problem arising from a failure to adapt to a threatening environment. It is culturally approved as it fits with a fast-moving, rapidly changing and demanding social environment. Being stressed is regarded almost as proof of membership of the club. The individual suffering from stress has to contend with a range of social attitudes about stress, some of which are in his favour and some against. In his favour is the growing awareness that employers have a duty of care to protect their employees from excessive stress because it can make them ill and can even be a cause of death. Good employers have always known how to look after their most valuable (and expensive) resources. For others it has taken the shock of a number of successful legal victories won by employees suing their employers for work-related stress. Against him is the stigma attached to someone who may be seen as 'not up to' the demands of the job/life. This failure to cope, when others apparently can, will negatively affect his job prospects.

The views which clients hold about their problems often make them less open to change. They may describe the problem in rigid, fixed terms. At some stage the counsellor needs to help the client to redefine the problem as being open to change and/or as only being temporary in nature. Some problems are clearly linked to transition stages and need to be seen in that context. They may, for example, occur around the time of a birth, in the months after a bereavement or a serious illness or in the early days after leaving home to go to university. Normalizing the experiences may help, as may the knowledge that these feelings, thoughts and behaviours are not permanent and will alter over time.

Deconstructing the problem

In the solution-focused approach all reality is socially negotiated through language. The counsellor will examine with the client how she is linguistically constructing her problem. This is to see if by using language in other ways will increase her chances of solving her problem. This process is called deconstruction and is defined by White (1993: 34) as

> procedures that subvert taken-for-granted realities and practices: those so-called 'truths' that are split off from the conditions and the context of their production; those disembodied ways of speaking that hide their biases and prejudices; and those familiar practices of self and of relationship that are subjugating people's lives.

Deconstructing the problem is not done in the more confrontational, psycho-educational style represented in some of the cognitive approaches. Among the most common techniques (O'Hanlon and Beadle, 1994) used by solution-focused counsellors and discussed in subsequent chapters are:

- looking for exceptions
- using action descriptions not labels
- depathologizing by changing labels

- framing difficulties as a stage
- normalizing
- externalizing the problem
- using metaphors and stories
- providing new frames of reference.

It is important that the deconstruction of the problem fits with the client's own values and perspectives. As counsellors we disclose the constructs, assumptions, biases and prejudices which comprise our own belief system as it meets the belief system of another human being. Yet despite these barriers the purpose of the encounter is to create a bridge between counsellor and client which will enable the client to explore the meaning of his or her life.

SKILLS REPERTOIRE

One way of reading clients' problems is to see them as a result of skills deficits on the part of the client. For example, the client has not learnt to stand up for himself, meet friends or commit himself to a relationship. If the client is going to overcome his difficulties he needs to learn and implement these skills. Some of these skills may be modelled in the counselling session, e.g. good communication or using humour. The practical acquisition of the relevant skill may form the negotiated goal for the client.

FAILED STRATEGIES

The founding members of Solution-Focused Therapy were strongly influenced by the brief therapy work undertaken at the Mental Research Institute (MRI) by people such as John Weakland, Richard Fisch and Paul Watzlawick. A fundamental tenet of the MRI approach is that problems are maintained by clients adopting failed-solution strategies. The failed solution becomes the problem; in order to change, clients need to abandon their failed solutions. To solve the problem they need to interrupt the recurring problem pattern and do something which is qualitatively different. For example, a parent may punish a child for bad behaviour but the child merely escalates the situation and invites further punishment. The punishments themselves then become an integral part of the problem situation. To break the vicious circle the parent needs to take a different line. For example, they could laugh at the situation, ignore the child (unless it is a safety issue) or give praise when the child does something right. Solution-focused practitioners have adopted the MRI principle of 'Do something different' to break out of a problem stalemate.

SOLUTION-FOCUSED PRINCIPLES

There are certain maxims which are standard components of the solution-focused model. They are practice guidelines which arise from the core beliefs.

KEEP THERAPY AS SIMPLE AS POSSIBLE

There is a commitment to work as economically and efficiently as possible. One way of accomplishing this is to resist beliefs and practices which complicate and inevitably prolong the process. These views may include:

- the solution needs to fit the problem
- the client is damaged, fragile, sick and in need of a cure
- the client's resources and competence are devalued
- the counsellor adopts an expert stance
- finding the reasons behind the client's problems is always helpful
- what the client thinks is the problem may not be the problem at all
- counselling will probably be long and painful
- the therapeutic alliance takes time to develop
- gains must be consolidated and worked through
- the client will probably get worse before he gets better and may even regress to a previous developmental stage
- interpretations must be based upon solid evidence gathered over time
- endings take time.

The solution-focused view is that such assumptions are likely to complicate the counselling relationship and intrude more into the client's personal space.

DO SOMETHING DIFFERENT

If you always do what you have always done, you will always get what you have got. Even for the client to stop and think about doing something different from normal may be enough to change it. Doing something different is an experiment which brings no guarantees. But if you want something to change the only way to do it is to change something. Talking about it is not enough. Doing something different can impact upon other significant people in the client's system and this in turn may produce different responses from them which reinforces the difference.

IF IT DOESN'T WORK STOP DOING IT

Repeating a failed solution blocks the client from making the kind of experiments necessary to move forward. Stopping what has not worked does not tell the client what to do instead but it does create a new set of circumstances in which they can explore what that something else could be. People under stress may be attached to repetitive behaviour which fails to deliver the desired result. The counsellor may seek to undermine such strategies or at least to invite the client to consider the advantages of giving them up and to support them as they search for alternatives. Failed stress management solutions include:

- Client uses more of the same type of solution. For example, they work even harder and get more tired, they make more mistakes and get more stressed. This is known as the hamster wheel solution!
- Client avoids doing what needs to be done – does not read letters from the bank,

throws bank statements in the rubbish bin. This is known as the ostrich solution!
* Client acts in ways which are irrelevant or inappropriate. For example, a client who drinks a bottle of whisky a day and one small sherry with his mother, gives up the sherry. This is known as the who do you think you're kidding solution!
* Client looks for perfect solutions. Since no solution is perfect, they do nothing but complain about their problem. This is known as the *mañana mañana* solution!

The principle of doing something different if current efforts are not working applies to the counsellor as well as to the client. During the first few sessions the counsellor will check out with the client whether what they are doing together is helpful to the client and, if so, how it is helpful and what difference it is making.

There is a strong belief in the solution-focused approach that the proof of the pudding is in the eating – where are the tangible results out there in the real world? Is the client beginning to see the kind of changes he wants? Is there a sense of moving forward and of heading in the right direction? How actively has the client engaged in work between the sessions? This constant evaluation is related to the client's stated goals. However, if no progress is taking place, the counsellor needs to ask herself whether she needs to adapt her approach and make changes. These may include:

* changing the pace of the work – either speeding up or slowing down
* listening to the problem more – being more empathic
* redefining the problem
* restating the goals
* being more active/less active
* revisiting the miracle answer
* reassessing the client's level of motivation and readiness for change
* reassessing whether the solution-focused approach suits this client.

If the counsellor decides, for whatever reason, a particular client cannot join with the solution-focused philosophy, the counsellor should be sufficiently flexible to change her style of work, perhaps using elements from other schools. This integrative approach will be discussed in Chapter 6. In some cases the counsellor may decide that a referral to another counsellor or a different form of counselling, for example, couple or group counselling, is appropriate. For some clients, it may be that they are currently unable to commit themselves to the demands of counselling and need to take a break and possibly return at a later date.

IF IT WORKS KEEP DOING IT

In the search for solutions clients will have reported a number of strategies which seem constructive and positive, although this may not be the way in which they are presented. After a period of failure, criticism and blame the client may have come to believe that nothing she does is right. In discussion with the counsellor the client will explore ways in which she could keep doing these strategies or even find ways of amplifying them. This principle is solidly based upon the fact that these strategies have been proven to lie within the client's repertoire and are potentially replicatable. Clients may require support and encouragement to build upon what might feel like fragile confidence. There may need to be a period of consolidation. Respecting and using the client's own pragmatic solutions frees the counsellor from the expert role in which she may be expected to think of original strategies which are previously untried by the client. As any counsellor knows, the attempt to 'sell' such strategies is often fruitless and ends in failure. Suggestions as to what the client might do may be accepted compliantly yet never acted upon. They may be dismissed as unsuitable for the client's circumstances (the 'Yes, but' game). Clients who ask for strategies tend to adopt them least. It is more effective to cooperate with the client's chosen solutions. The client is unlikely to resist and having his affirmed can be an empowering experience. Knowing they are on the right track and already doing things which are helpful will come as a welcome relief to the stressed client who had lost confidence in his own judgement.

IF IT ISN'T BROKEN, DON'T FIX IT

The solution-focused counsellor sees the client as having various gifts, talents, experiences, values and beliefs which can potentially be part of the solution. It is crucial that clients get in touch with the parts of their lives which are healthy and functioning well. 'There is nothing wrong with you that what is right with you cannot fix.' The principle 'if it isn't broken, don't fix it' is a warning to counsellors not to presume they have carte blanche to enquire about every aspect of a client's life. There is a growing tendency for professionals to therapize people unnecessarily, that is to label normal human unhappiness as pathological and therefore requiring professional assistance. The solution-focused approach stands in opposition to such a trend. It often expresses scepticism as to whether something is a problem at all and, if it is, for whom is it a problem? It is more likely to normalize problems as part of the human condition.

CHAPTER 3

The Solution-Focused Process

The solution-focused approach is non-directive in terms of client goals and outcomes but the counsellor plays the leading role in directing the process itself. The next few chapters will describe and explain the key interventions used. In this chapter we consider how the component parts come together.

SOLUTION-FOCUSED STRUCTURE

I have divided the structure of the process into:

- problem talk
- future talk
- strategy talk.

In Figure 3.1 we can see that in terms of the balance of time the greater amount is spent in future and strategy talk than in problem talk. Through the use of coping questions such as 'How did you get through that?' it is possible to engage in strategy talk while the client is relating the problem narrative. There is an overlap between the three processes. It is this attention to the future and to the resources of the client which distinguishes this approach from others.

Problem talk

Contrary to the myths about solution-focused therapy counsellors do attend to clients' problems. They listen to their problems for as long as the clients need them to do so. The counsellor uses the following interventions:

Figure 3.1 *The solution-focused process*

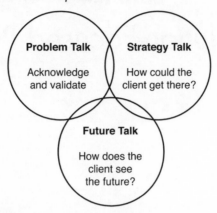

ACKNOWLEDGE AND VALIDATE THE PROBLEM

To build the therapeutic alliance successfully the client needs to feel that his concerns have been heard and understood by the counsellor. Whichever problem the client presents is the immediate focus for the work. The focus may subsequently change in later sessions.

INVITE THE CLIENT TO PUT THE PROBLEM INTO ONE WORD AND THAT WORD INTO ONE SENTENCE

This technique, borrowed from Multi Modal Therapy (Lazarus, 1981), does not strictly belong in the solution–focused repertoire. However, it often helps the client to focus quickly on priority issues. This focus is essential for therapy to be brief. Not all clients can answer the question precisely but most are able to use it as a starting point.

Counsellor:	Could you put your problem into one word?
Client:	Frustrated.
Counsellor:	Could you put that word into one sentence?
Client:	I feel frustrated because I have no energy. I am permanently tired.

CONVERT THE PROBLEM INTO WELL-FORMED GOALS

Once the counsellor has this information she converts the problem statement into an achievable goal.

Counsellor:	If counselling was helpful you would feel less tired all of the time and you would have more energy.
Client:	Yes.
Counsellor:	What would you be doing when you had more energy?
Client:	I would stay awake in the evening. I would watch less television and do something more interesting like an evening class. I would concentrate better at work and feel more enthusiastic about my job.

The counsellor then explores whether any of these activities have happened recently.

USE ACTION DESCRIPTIONS NOT LABELS (O'HANLON AND BEADLE, 1994)

The client may use a script which he has learnt from professionals. This script will use the vocabulary currently in vogue, for example, 'attention deficit disorder' or 'borderline personality'. These abstract labels act as shorthand for categories of people. They conceal a range of values, interests and prejudices. The solution-focused counsellor seeks to discover the unique personal meaning these abstract labels hold for the client. By eliciting specific descriptions of what the client means when he uses terms such as depression, the counsellor grounds the conversation in the uniqueness of the client's experience.

EXAMPLE

Client:　　I am suffering from anxiety.
Counsellor:　Could you tell me what happens when you feel anxious?
Client:　　I worry about everything. I cannot eat for worrying. I do not want to be in the company of other people.
Counsellor:　What else shows you that you are feeling anxious?
Client:　　I lie in bed at night worrying about the next day and I am exhausted in the morning.

The concrete description also suggests the changes which the clients would like to see. He would worry less. He would eat sensibly. He would choose whether to be with others or on their own. Breaking a solid problem into manageable processes helps the client to be hopeful that change is possible. While labels are sometimes helpful they can also foster resignation and passivity. Some labels give the client a problem identity for life. For example, a diagnosis of alcoholism can be a life sentence. Society likes to have snappy labels for every human experience even when they are oppressive. The solution-focused counsellor is likely to avoid the problem label the client brings and instead talk about what the client would like to see happening in his life.

Language borrowed from the medical and psychiatric worlds can foreclose options for the client. It can lock the client into the medical/psychiatric system. The aim in solution-focused therapy is to help clients to move beyond the absence of illness to the recovery of their lives. Recovering a life means reawakening all those things which make life worth living.

Labels turn fluid and evolving processes into apparently fixed conditions. Labels give the appearance of reality to words such as stress or depression. In the real world however there is no such 'thing' as stress or depression. They are linguistic expressions constructed within a social context. What is labelled as mental illness in one culture is constructed as mystical experience in another. Behaviour which contemporary culture defines as illness was viewed as immorality or criminality by our ancestors.

ADAPT COUNSELLING STYLE TO MATCH THE CLIENT

The counsellor seeks to cooperate with the client. She will ask, 'How can I be helpful to you?' Initially the client may not be able to answer this clearly. He may say that he wants to talk to someone who is independent. He may want to sound out the counsellor to confirm what he already thinks or is planning to do. He may want the counsellor to listen or to generate ideas. He may have had a positive experience with another counsellor and would like to repeat the experience. In the solution-focused approach, as distinct from the psychodynamic, the counsellor will not give importance to issues of transference. In the opening stages the counsellor will:

- ask how it feels for the client to come for counselling
- find out about his previous experiences of seeking help
- go slowly and gently and not pressurize the client
- allow the client time to tell his story without being interrupted
- reassure the client about confidentiality
- give the client the opportunity to ask questions
- explain carefully the method of counselling and number of sessions on offer
- ask questions to help the client to make a start if necessary
- acknowledge the client's distress
- be active in communicating empathy
- assess the client's ability to form a relationship
- assess the client's awareness of his own resources
- assess the client's expectations of the counsellor.

When the client makes a request for the counsellor to help in a certain way the counsellor will ask how that would be helpful for the client. For example, if the client felt that he had been listened to, it would help him to be decisive.

NEGOTIATE PROBLEM DEFINITION

What happens at this stage of problem negotiation is crucial for therapeutic outcome. If the counsellor allows the client to define the problem as insolvable then failure is guaranteed. The skill lies in staying close to the client's definition of the problem while translating it into one which is open to solutions.

Future talk

All conversations are 'joint productions' with each participant shaping and being shaped by the rules of the conversation (turn taking) and the social behaviour of the other person. The counsellor, by virtue of her role, is the conversation manager. The kind of conversation the counsellor encourages, invites, reinforces and rewards is likely to prevail. A solution-focused counsellor will foster a future orientation to the conversation and the client will, if the timing is right, join her. A client may not be able to sustain the future perspective for long. It is as if the client begins by looking at the ground and the counsellor is looking upwards to the sky. Inevitably the client is drawn into looking up to see what the counsellor (figuratively) finds so interesting up there. As Oscar Wilde said, 'We are all in the gutter but some of us are looking at the stars.'

It is also characteristic of the solution-focused conversation that, although the tone and tenor is set by the counsellor, once the client has been recruited into solution-focused talk, the counsellor's interventions closely follow the client's preceding statements. Apart from the introduction of specific interventions, such as the miracle question or scaling, the counsellor stays very close to the client's process.

EXAMPLE

Client:	I would like the world to stop so I could get off for a break.
Counsellor:	How would you want to use that break?
Client:	I would do absolutely nothing.
Counsellor:	You mean you would have time to think or just be?
Client:	I do not want to think. I want to switch off altogether.
Counsellor:	That sounds good.
Client:	I feel that my mind is racing all the time. It would be lovely to just blank out.
Counsellor:	I think I can see why that sounds good to you. How would it be helpful for you?
Client:	I could stop being responsible for everyone all of the time. I would have more of my own life back.
Counsellor:	When that starts to happen for you what will be the first sign?
Client:	I will work less, sleep more and have fun.

The future orientation is one of the lenses used by the counsellor to explore the client's story. It is one which clients are often pleased to engage with, once the initial problem validation phase has been accomplished. Solution-focused techniques such as the miracle question and scaling are useful for drawing out the big picture and the small steps which comprise the client's hopes for the future.

Strategy talk

Having clarified with the client where she or he would like to get to, the next step is to explore the steps to get there. The solution-focused counsellor elicits from clients those strategies which work for them. In exploring strategies the counsellor follows the principle of utilization.

UTILIZATION

This principle and its application in the solution-focused approach derives from the work of Milton Erickson. Utilization means that the counsellor uses anything the client brings to the therapy. This could include conscious and unconscious factors, resources, experiences, abilities, hobbies, relationships, attitudes, problems and deficits (Zeig and Munion, 1999). Highlighting the uniqueness of each individual in this way ensures each therapeutic encounter is itself unique. Theories are left at the door of the counselling room and the client holds centre stage. The client becomes the pivot around which a working therapeutic model is devised. The model fits the unique human being in the presence of the counsellor. Nothing about the person is without value or relevance to the work. All aspects of the client are included. Everything the client says or does is useful. The solution–focused counsellor uses an inclusive approach which affirms the client as a competent person.

Most forms of counselling subscribe to the utilization of clients' resources as part of the therapeutic process. Rogers (1961), for example, portrayed people as basically healthy. In his view they had an in-built tendency towards using their potential, towards achieving 'self-actualization'. It is difficult to see how counselling could work otherwise. One does not build a house on sand, one needs strong foundations. The bases for change are the client's competence, qualities and strengths, values and skills. The British Association for Counselling Code for Counsellors (1998) describes the overall aim of counselling as being 'to provide an opportunity for the client to work towards living in a more satisfying and resourceful way ... the counsellor's role is to facilitate the client's work in ways which respect the client's values, personal resources and capacity for self determination'. Although this attention to client resources is a common factor across the board, it occupies a more central role in the solution–focused approach than in any other. In problem-focused therapies attention to the client's resources can be outweighed by an interest in psychopathology, which obscures the view of the client as resourceful. Of course many clients collude with or actively seek a problem identity. At times having a label can come as a relief however unsatisfactory it is. Some forms of assessment, however, are so preoccupied with pathology, client deficits, weaknesses, maladaptive behaviour and illness that they fail to give clients any credit for their resourcefulness. This is an unhelpful imbalance. Recent research has suggested that clients are much more resilient than the therapy culture insinuates. Most people actually feel that they become stronger rather than weaker after a tragic experience (Tedeschi *et al.*, 1999).

Figure 3.2 *Solution-focused strategy questions*

What ideas have you got about this?
What ideas have you considered, but rejected or are still thinking about?
What needs to happen about them?
What ideas have you thought about but perhaps not fully worked out how to put into practice?
Do you have some ideas which it might be helpful to share with someone before you put them into action?
Does anyone else who knows you well have any ideas what you could do?
If that option isn't available to you what is?
What strengths do you have which you could utilize?
What past experiences contain important lessons which are transferable?
What do your exceptions teach you about your capacity to overcome life's challenges?
Which stress-reducing strategies fit you?

BEGINNINGS

Contracting

Solution-focused counselling offers a partnership in which the client determines the start and the endpoint and the counsellor takes responsibility for the route to be travelled. The route will normally offer the client choices at each signpost along the way. In order to construct a genuinely client-centred agenda the counsellor asks:

- What would you like to focus on today?
- When you were thinking about the session was there something you wanted to make sure we worked on?
- What is most important for you to talk about today?
- What changes are you thinking of making?
- What makes you feel that now is a good time to change?
- Of the various concerns that you have at the moment where would you like to start?
- Is there one part of this problem which, if solved, would help other parts?

The counsellor wants the client to feel safe and relaxed. She wants him to feel that it was a good idea to come. The tone of the initial exchanges depends upon the client's previous experience of counselling. In order to join with the client the counsellor will enquire what was helpful about the experience. If it was positive the counsellor will want to incorporate the successful elements. If it was negative the counsellor will want to avoid making the same mistakes.

The counsellor accepts the client's presenting problem as a good starting point and begins to negotiate goals for the work.

> The presenting problem offers, in one package, what the patient is ready to work on, a concentrated manifestation of whatever is wrong, and a concrete index of any progress made. (Weakland, *et al.*, 1974: 147)

Problem-free talk

The solution-focused approach encourages a period of problem-free talk with the client (George *et al.*, 1990). This is a preliminary informal conversation which attempts to set the client at ease while at the same time finding out about aspects of his or her life which could be helpful when constructing solutions. The conversation is often about what the client enjoys doing when the problem is not so great or about some activity which the client is good at. The conversation often reveals client qualities, interests, preferences, values and strategies which the counsellor can tap into later. For example, knowing that someone likes fishing may tell us that:

- they can organize and plan
- they can tolerate/enjoy their own company
- they have a certain amount of patience and tenacity
- they use information in a practical way

- they like the outdoors
- they like peace and quiet
- they have found and carried out an activity which relaxes them.

Pre-session change

From the initial contact the counsellor focuses on the theme of change. The counsellor communicates to the client her conviction that change is inevitable, that it is already taking place and will continue. The counsellor explains she works as a brief therapist and for most clients this will mean a relatively small number of sessions – on average three or four. There will usually be an option to extend this number where necessary. If the client does not experience some change and improvement within the first few sessions then there needs to be a review to decide (a) whether the problem needs to be redefined, (b) whether the goals are appropriate and clear enough or need to be renegotiated, (c) whether the strategies need to be adapted to fit the client, (d) whether the style of the therapist or her timing and pacing needs to be adjusted, (e) whether the time scales need to be revised, (f) whether counselling is an appropriate intervention for this client at this point in time or (g) whether a referral to another agency or counsellor would be appropriate.

In the first session the counsellor engages the client as an active agent in her own therapy by asking her to notice any changes which take place between the time of making the appointment and the first session (pre-session change). The counsellor asks about these changes when they meet. Weiner-Davis *et al.* (1987) in their research on pre-session change discovered that 66 per cent of a selected group of clients reported positive pre-session changes. Lawson (1994) in replicating this research found that 62 per cent of clients reported positive change. Clients who recall positive pre-session change have already begun to identify for themselves exceptions to the problem. They have begun to recognize what they have or have not done to bring about change. This 'flying start' stimulates an impetus for change. It builds confidence, increases hope and sets the tone for future exchanges.

Clients welcome the recognition from the counsellor that they have assets in their personal banks. They may have felt stigmatized and deskilled in seeking help. There may have been pressures from others to see their situation as failure and inadequacy.

EXAMPLE

Counsellor: Have you noticed any differences since you contacted me last week?
Client: When I phoned you I was stressed out of mind. I felt desperate. I could not sleep or work.
Counsellor: So what got you through till today?
Client: My partner has been great. He just listened to me for hours.
Counsellor: So it feels better when you talk about it to someone who understands.
Client: I do not know if he really understands. But he listens and he gets me to do something else to relax me.
Counsellor: Such as?
Client: Sometimes just take a rest or watch television.
Counsellor: Does it help to switch off for a while?

Client:	Easier said than done. I sometimes feel my head is going to explode.
Counsellor:	What has helped you to switch off even for a short time?
Client:	I deliberately tell myself I am not getting paid for thinking about work. Why should I give them that time? I think about the holiday we had or a film I have been to or I read the paper instead.
Counsellor:	What else have you found that fights the stress?
Client:	I decided not to take any work home for the next few weeks. I found that really hard but I managed to do it.

Clients may be reluctant to give themselves credit or may explain progress as temporary or coincidental. For the counsellor to try and persuade or 'cheerlead' the client is likely to be counterproductive. A better strategy is to express continuing curiosity about the changes and to suggest that 'something must have happened,' 'What do you think it was?' Clients can feel unsure about change because they do not know whether it will continue or they are unsure whether they have the resources to maintain it. While some people struggle to make a start others are keen starters but lack the stamina and perseverance to keep going when initial enthusiasm flags (the twin enemies of inertia and entropy) (Egan, 1998).

Visitor, complainant and customer

Table 3.1 *Visitor, complainant and customer*

Position	Owns problem	Ready to change
Visitor	No	No
Complainant	Yes	No
Customer	Yes	Yes

De Shazer (1988a) uses the terms *visitor, complainant* and *customer* to distinguish different types of relationships between clients and counsellors. The *visitor* relationship is one in which the client is sent by someone – the court, his employer or partner, for example. Sometimes the client attends under threat of negative consequences if he does not. There may be an ethical issue for the counsellor in relation to the degree of consent the client has given. The visitor is a person who does not think he has a problem and neither wants to be in counselling nor believes it can help with his problem. His aim is to get someone off his back and to leave counselling as soon as possible. Such interviews can be unproductive unless the counsellor can find something which the client wants and which the counsellor can help with. Berg (1991) argues that when the client has low motivation and sees no connection between his situation and what he thinks the counsellor can do, the counsellor's task is:

- to join the client's world view
- to find ways to influence the client so that he can identify problems and possible solutions to them

- to agree as far as possible with the client's idea about the problem.

During the session the counsellor will listen respectfully and be empathic, cooperative and positive. If there is an opportunity to compliment the client they will do so. Should she elicit a goal from the client she will ask solution-oriented questions such as:

- What would need to happen for your manager/social worker/partner to change their mind about you and stop giving you a hard time?
- Are you interested in doing that?
- Could you do it?
- How would you do it?
- What difference would that make to you if you did it?
- How do you think anyone else would respond?
- How long do you think you could keep it up?
- When/How would you know it was a good time to try that?

If the client asks for help the counsellor cannot give, she can respond by saying, 'If I cannot help you with that, is there anything else I can help you with?' On occasion the counsellor may convert a visitor into a customer. Meeting someone who is trying to cooperate with his goals and is not pushing another agenda could lower the client's usual defences and lead to a genuine request for help. At least the client has had a caring experience and may be encouraged to use counselling at a later date when he is motivated to make changes. In order to save time and resources however, the counsellor would be advised not to try to persuade a visitor to occupy the customer role.

A *complainant* relationship is one in which the client is willing to explore the problem but does not see himself as having a part to play in constructing the solution. He may engage in extended problem talk about an absent third party who is perceived to have power and control in the situation. The client may perceive himself as a passive victim of fate with little power to change. Such clients may be resigned or despairing about the future. Hawkes *et al.* (1998) suggest the counsellor should ask such clients whether they think it is realistic to think that they could change the person they are complaining about. Further questions might be, 'Given that this situation is going to continue (or this other person is not going to change) how could you make life better for yourself? If you were to take one small step forward for yourself what do you think it would be?'

A client could be a complainant in respect of one aspect of his problem and a customer in another.

EXAMPLE

David was grossly overworked by his employer. He had no influence over his working life. Every minute was controlled by his employer. He was bound by the terms of a new contract which he was pressurized into signing. In this aspect of his life he felt unable to make changes. In his personal life, however, he worked hard to improve his relationship with his son with whom he had been having major conflict.

Where the client is in a complainant relationship the counsellor listens empathically, finds ways to match the client's language and frame of reference and compliments him on his concern to find a way to change. Complainants may be invited to gather information about exceptions.

A *customer* relationship is one in which the client recognizes that there is a problem over which he has some control and he is ready and willing to do something about it. The client actively seeks to engage the counsellor in a search for solutions. There may be immediate circumstances which act as an incentive to change. These spurs to action may be an impending threat, 'unless you get your act together, this relationship is over' or a clear benefit to be gained, 'if I control my anxiety at work I may get promoted'. It can be helpful to ask the client what has been happening recently that led them to think counselling would be a good idea. A client may have had a problem for a long time and could have sought help at any point but for some reason they feel now is the right time.

The change process

WHAT TO CHANGE?

It can be difficult to know where to start when faced with a complex patchwork of problems. Is one part of a problem a better starting point than others? Where is the leverage (Egan, 1990)? Which part of the problem does the person feel most capable/hopeful about changing? It is common sense to start with a prospect of success as early failure is likely to dent the client's confidence for future changes. As well as being clear about what the client *does* want to change, it is helpful to remember what he does not want to change.

HOW DO YOU RECOGNIZE THE SIGNS OF CHANGE?

Having an end vision can help but in order to keep going people need signs of progress which sustain them and make their efforts worthwhile. These signs need to be identified and actively sought by the client. If clients are at first unable to do these tasks, they need to work on it between sessions. Clients may have other difficulties about the change process. The following questions may need to be asked by the counsellor:

1. Does the client want to change?

The Cycle of Change Model (Prochaska *et al.*, 1992) describes five stages of a cycle through which people go as they try to change their behaviour. The five stages are:

- Pre-contemplation
  The person is a reluctant or involuntary client with little or no genuine motivation. Someone else may want them to change or they may feel powerless in the face of the challenge. The stress they are under may have undermined their confidence, their judgement, their decisiveness and their capacity for action.

- Contemplation
  At one level the client in the contemplation stage wants to make changes but on another level there is a belief that the timing is not right and they lack the commitment to make a start.
- Preparation
  At this point in the cycle the client is thinking seriously about how to overcome his problem. He may have taken preparatory steps to clear the way for decisive action. He is ready to go.
- Action
  The client has begun to implement his plan.
- Maintenance
  In this stage the client continues to maintain the changes he has initiated but may also have setbacks and relapses. He needs strategies to recover and keep on track. A solution-focused approach is able to contribute to all these stages in the cycle.

2. Does the client know how to change?

Even with clear motivation the client may not know where to start. As one client said, 'It has helped coming for counselling. I knew where I wanted to get to but I had so many problems I just did not know where to start.'

3. Is the client aware of obstacles to change?

Perhaps one of the dangers in being solution-focused is that the counsellor can become too partisan in fighting for change, to the extent that the difficulties to be overcome are underestimated. For some clients at the contemplation or action stage of the cycle change is more like a sprint but for others it is a marathon. Being prepared to tackle obstacles, failures, setbacks and recurring bouts of hopelessness makes ultimate success more likely. The solution-focused counsellor will ensure that the client is a self-advocate for change and will ask questions to elicit her reasons for making changes.

EXAMPLE

Counsellor:	It sounds as if there are some benefits for you in being off sick. What makes you think it is a good idea to go back to work?
Client:	The longer I am off, the harder it will be to go back. I miss some of the people anyway. I do not want to be sitting around at home all day.
Counsellor:	So how will you know when is a good time to go back?
Client:	I'll know. My partner will tell me when she thinks I'm ready. When the doctor signs me off, I will have an interview with personnel and see what they say.

4. Is the client confident about making changes?

Levels of confidence fluctuate. The counsellor may need to work on building the client's confidence slowly by helping him to take small steps forward. As confidence grows the goals can be expanded.

5. Is the client ready to make changes?

Stress can make people stop and re-evaluate their lives and make decisions about the future. They may have needed an illness or redundancy to force them off the merry-go-round and to give them the time and space they need to think. For some clients there is a heavy price to pay for change. Some choices isolate the person from their family, peer group or community. Changes may bring benefits in the short term but may have detrimental effects in the long term. Clients do not have any guarantees that the proposed changes will work. It is not possible to predict exactly what the consequences of change might be. There can be unexpected side effects.

Clients who feel unsure or stigmatized about seeking help need reassurance from the counsellor that they will not be pressurized prematurely into change nor will they be expected to pursue counsellor-inspired 'solutions' which they feel are unattainable, irrelevant or undesirable. A premature rush towards solutions by the counsellor is likely to encounter resistance. Moving too fast may lead to the development of ill-considered solutions which do not work in the long run.

MIDDLE STAGE

The key activity in second and subsequent sessions of counselling is the continuing identification and amplification of significant changes. The process is summed up in the acronym EARS proposed by the Brief Family Therapy Centre (Berg, 1994):

Elicit change
Amplify
Reinforce
Start over again

Elicit change

The counsellor seeks news of difference, 'What's different since we last met?' She resets the focus on change, 'What changes have you noticed?' There is a strong lead from the counsellor at this point in setting the tone of the session. There is no invitation to develop problem talk. If the client reports problems then the counsellor listens attentively and empathically. The counsellor encourages the client to concentrate more on what has worked than what has not worked. When changes are reported the counsellor ensures the client receives the credit. In addition, the counsellor explores with the client the details of how she managed to make the change. 'How did you do that? How did it start?' This enquiry will focus upon (a) the sequence of behaviours which led to the new behaviour, (b) the difference in thinking which preceded and accompanied it and (c) any feelings associated with having accomplished it.

Amplify

In the next step the counsellor asks the client about the effects of these changes and the learning which has arisen from them. He will use questions such as:

- How did you work out what to do?
- Was that your idea or did you get it from someone else?
- How did your partner/parent/boss/friend react when you did/said that?
- What happened after that?
- What does making this change say about you?
- What has it made you think of doing next?

Reinforce

The counsellor supports the client in her change-making providing that the changes are genuinely leading her towards her agreed goals. If they are creating other problems as a by-product these also need to be addressed. The counsellor helps clients to see how her changes might be perceived by other significant parties. Counsellors reinforce change both in their verbal and non-verbal responses to the client. The former may include compliments and specific comments relating to the strengths and qualities that the client used, for example, 'That must have taken a lot of ... courage/imagination/perseverance'. On occasion the counsellor underlines this by telling the client that 'many other people could not have managed to do what you did'. Compliments of this kind are well received by most clients, as long as they are not of a patronizing nature and are offered in a transparently genuine way by the counsellor. Non-verbal reinforcement comes from the counsellor's body language – smiles, nods, handshakes and minimal prompts (the 'Wow' response, for which Anglo-Saxon English does not have an exact equivalent!).

Start over again

Once the counsellor has fully explored a reported change, she will invite the client to consider whether there have been any other changes. 'So what else is better?' Again the body language of the counsellor is important. If she looks as if she expects the client to have something else to report there is a far greater chance that the client will think of other change events. If the question is asked with little positive curiosity the answer is likely to be in the negative.

As the client returns for further sessions the counsellor regularly reviews progress:

- Is this counselling being helpful to you?
- Is this what you expected?
- Of the things we have talked about so far what has been most helpful to you?
- What difference is it making in your life?
- How is it affecting other people?
- What have you learned about yourself through coming here?

The counsellor may use some of the techniques, such as the stress map or scaling, described in Chapters 5 and 6.

ENDINGS

Endings should always be on the agenda from the beginning. Counsellors should aim to remove themselves from the client's life as soon as possible, as soon as the client is confident that they can carry on the changes they have begun, otherwise there is the danger of dependency and loss of focus. An agency which offers ongoing support to clients has to define it in such a way that it does not become confused with goal-directed counselling.

In solution-focused counselling clients define the goals of counselling and largely determine when counselling should end. Scaling is a useful tool for clarifying endings. The counsellor asks the client what will be good enough for her on a scale of 0–10, with 0 being the *status quo* and 10 being the morning after a miracle. She then invites him to describe what will be happening or not happening when he has reached the desired point on the scale. It is crucial that there is a clear agreement as to what will constitute the signs of ending. Without such definition it is very difficult to monitor progress. In all forms of counselling endings need preparation.

CHAPTER 4

First Steps

Although there is a structure in solution-focused work it is a flexible one. Describing the following interventions as first steps is therefore misleading in that they need not necessarily precede interventions described in the next chapter as second steps. The order or sequence in which interventions are made varies from client to client and is dependent upon the judgement of the counsellor at the time. An experienced counsellor is often unaware of how the different strands are interwoven during a session. It is only in supervision or in listening to a recording of the interview that the process becomes clear. Counselling is much more of an art than a science. If the practitioner adopts an integrative stance, interventions which originate in other schools of therapy, for example, cognitive behavioural, have their own rationale for being included in the solution-focused process.

BEGINNINGS

The counsellor engages the client in a conversation about the client's changing experience of the problem. In doing so, the counsellor seeks to understand the client's concerns, while at the same time listening for information about the client's competence.

When the conversation is more about solutions than problems, there is often a release of energy in the room. Talking about solutions makes them more real. It expands their reality. In eliciting solution talk the counsellor becomes a witness to the client's qualities, strengths and hopes for the future. The content and flavour of the counsellor's questions may surprise clients who expected a problem-oriented dialogue. Clients are often struck by the kind of questions they are being asked and begin to see their problem in a new light. In conventional problem-focused exploration clients may go into a downward spiral as they expand on the problem. Excessive dwelling on problems can, at least initially, set people back. In the solution-focused approach the task of the counsellor is not to uncover the lost 'truth' which will explain the client's current problems - the 'counsellor as psychological detective' model – but to create a climate in which the client finds a voice to express their experience and have their strengths and competence affirmed. This hearing has been denied those whose view of the world has been devalued, dismissed or suppressed. By focusing upon interactions – the journey outwards – rather than upon intrapsychic phenomena – the journey inwards – solution-focused counselling acknowledges the client's perspectives as having legitimacy in a public context. Counselling becomes an exercise in generating alternative attitudes, interpretations, choices and strategies.

The counsellor first listens attentively to the client's concerns and acknowledges and validates them. This listening lasts as long as it takes the client to experience understanding and empathy from the counsellor. Some clients need longer than others to tell their story or to feel trusting towards the counsellor. The entire first session or first few sessions may consist of the counsellor listening to the client's concerns and issues in a respectful way. Clients need to feel safe with the counsellor before they feel confident enough to explore future scenarios. For the solution-focused counsellor the therapeutic alliance is a respectful collaborative stance, oriented towards client goals. The solution-focused view is that a warm, supportive and positive relationship is important for purposeful cooperation but is not sufficient in itself to generate the changes the client wants. The relationship is a means to an end not an end in itself. Normally the relationship is not the focus of attention between the counsellor and the client. The counsellor may use supervision to reflect upon the relationship with the client and to consider ways in which it could be improved. As the client begins to experience progress, the relationship becomes a close working partnership. There is a mixture of ingredients in the relationship such as encouragement, reassurance, humour, affirmation and celebration. Respecting what the client wants, provided it is lawful and ethical, and joining with the client in working towards it is the central and only agenda.

GOAL SETTING

In McDonald's (1994) study of Solution-Focused Therapy in a National Health service clinic there was a significant correlation between positive outcome and the successful negotiation of specific goals for treatment. The outcome was less successful when goals were defined negatively and least successful when the goals were non-specific. In order to keep on track – to keep the focus – appropriate goals need to be formulated as clearly as possible. Goals should not become obsessions. For some clients their high level of stress has a lot to do with an excessive emphasis on meeting targets, achieving goals and measuring performance. In the counselling relationship itself, such clients may unconsciously replicate a similar drive towards achieving results in order to gain the approval of the counsellor. Counsellors need to be aware of this, otherwise the compulsive achiever will set out to prove that she is the 'client of the year' and counselling will become part of the problem rather than part of the solution. Sometimes clients just ask the counsellor to listen, 'to get it off my chest', and often feel better for having done so. For some clients being listened to is enough to make a difference. Clients who suffer from work-related stress often complain that their managers never listen to them, even when they are begging for extra help or resources to do their job. The managers may not want to hear because they themselves are highly stressed and feel guilty they are not protecting their colleagues from unacceptable pressure. They are then uncomfortable about being confronted with the inevitable consequences of their actions upon subordinates. Their impotence is a major stressor for them. Stress is passed down the chain until one of the links breaks. When the client comes to see a stress counsellor she may need time and space to voice her long-suppressed thoughts and feelings about her situation and to receive reassurance that she is not, as she may fear, going mad.

The solution-focused approach aims to stay close to the client's stated goals. This pragmatic and purposeful fit between counsellor and client encourages the client as she experiences a clear sense of purpose and progress. It is the task of the counsellor to help the client to form clear, simple, attainable goals appropriate for counselling. Clients often present with goals which belong in other arenas – financial services, legal advice, housing enquiries, mediation, career guidance. These services may be available to the client through Employee Assistance Programmes. Counselling can complement these other forms of support. I have worked with clients on emotional and psychological difficulties resulting from stress, while their trade union has supported them in grievance or disciplinary hearings and an advisor is helping them with their financial or legal problems. Clients, counsellors and other agencies need to be clear about the boundaries of counselling. It is normally the case, for example, that the counsellor will not give advice or act as an advocate for his client.

In the current climate when many clients have been 'sent' by the courts, their employers or other agencies, it is not always easy to find goals which the client owns and is willing to work on, which are compatible with the goals of the commissioning referrer. There may also be pressure on the client to prove that counselling has produced the result required by the referrer. Frank, for example, was warned by his employer that counselling was his last chance; if he did not change as a result of it, he would be sacked. Goals need to match the motivation and response-ability of the client. For some people, the threat of sanctions may galvanize them into action, for others, the promise of rewards is more likely to motivate them. In either case, the goals must confer a clear benefit upon the client sufficient to sustain their often painful efforts to change.

The counsellor attempts to clarify with the client what they hope will be happening should counselling be successful. This is not always possible from the outset, as many people under stress cannot 'see the wood for the trees', and find it difficult to articulate the kind of changes they want. They may feel confused, vague, unsettled; perhaps mystified as to what is troubling them and are unable to put their problem easily into words. If they are depressed, or if there are no successes or achievements in their memory bank, they will have limited vision of a better quality of life and no sense of their own power to make it happen. Some preliminary work may need to be done before they can believe they have any control and choice. The following questions can begin to explore a client's expectations:

- How long do you think it will take before things start to improve?
- How many times do you think we will need to meet?
- How will you know that it was worthwhile coming for counselling?
- What will start/stop happening in your life?
- What will be the first signs for you that things are going in the right direction?

The counsellor can ask the client what his expectations are about the length of time they will need to meet. This can result in surprising answers because many clients want fewer sessions than the counsellor is willing to give them (Pekarik and Wierzbicki, 1986).

The solution-focused approach aims for incremental changes – small steps in the right direction, 'If you could take only one small step in the right direction in the next couple of days, what would it be?' (Dolan, 1998). Of course, goals can shift throughout the duration of the counselling and both parties need to evaluate constantly the validity of the original goals and be clear when they require modification or replacement. In brief or time-limited work it is essential that the goals be realistic for the time available. However, even where the client's goals are unrealistic and unattainable, the counsellor can respect the good intentions behind them and try to utilize them. The client need not achieve all her goals in the one course of counselling, she could prioritize and take time out of the relationship to experiment and consolidate her progress before returning to counselling at a later stage.

The counsellor will use his skills to assist the client in shaping realistic goals. For Egan (1994), 'A goal is realistic if the client has access to the resources needed to accomplish it, external circumstances do not prevent its accomplishment, the goal is under the client's control, the goal is sustainable and the benefits outweigh the costs' (p. 261). Empowering goals tend to meet the following criteria:

1. *Grounded.* The more grounded or concrete the goal – the more it can be pictured in the mind's eye – the easier it is to focus upon it. For example, instead of 'I would like to sort my head out', which is too vague to be helpful, a more specific description would be elicited, 'I would know when I was starting to get really irritated before I lost my temper' or 'I would get things more in proportion'.
2. *Simple and clear.* Goals need to be as clear as possible, not ambiguous, vague or complicated.
3. *Measurable.* Not everything in life can be measured but it does help to know whether a goal is or is not being reached and, if not, how out of reach it is. It is hard to have a sense of direction unless there are signposts along the way.
4. *In keeping with the client's values.* Respecting the values of the client, provided they are legal and ethical, ensures that the negotiated goals fit the client's world view. The counsellor may need to be aware of potential conflict between the values of short-term and long-term consequences, for example a short-term goal may be to leave a relationship but the long-term result may be ostracization from one's family or community.

With some clients it can be useful to use a goal attainment chart in order to monitor progress.

This is a chart recording Jo's work as she seeks to reduce her stress levels. The chart is filled in by the client not the counsellor. The chart reveals that there was an immediate impact following the first session. Jo said that she was desperate for help when she came and that just making the effort to do something about it was a powerful trigger for her to take action. She decided she had to take control of her life. Following the first session, she reported that she had done the following:

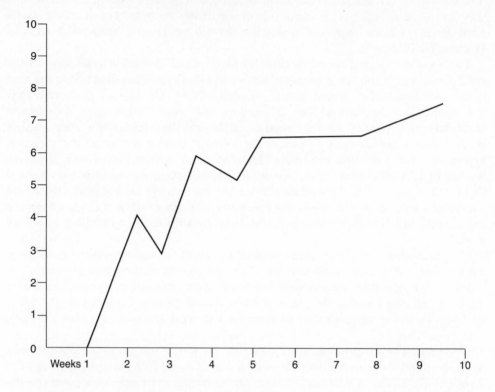

- on two occasions she had spent fifteen minutes on her own doing relaxation exercises
- stopped drinking alcohol at lunch
- been for a walk at the weekend
- had an early night
- listened to her most relaxing music
- tried to listen better when her children were telling her stories about their day at school and helped them with their homework.

Following the second session, there was something of a relapse as Jo came under a lot of pressure at work before she had been able to establish her new routines. In addition, she had a serious argument with her partner at home, which meant that home did not feel like a friendly sanctuary for a while. Between weeks three and four this conflict was resolved and home became a more therapeutic environment again. There were some good times with her partner and children – going to the cinema together and having a day out in town. It had been quite some time since this had happened. There had also been some very enjoyable lovemaking during this period, which always made her feel much better about herself. Life seemed to be improving and she was handling work situations much more confidently. By session six, the situation had stabilized. After two more sessions of consolidation Jo felt ready to end the counselling.

EXCEPTION SEEKING

One of the key interventions in solution-focused stress counselling is the seeking of exceptions (de Shazer *et al.*, 1986) to the stress. Finding times when the stress was absent or was more manageable can be helpful in reframing clients' understandings of their circumstances and options (Miller, 1997). Freedman and Combs (1993) describe seeking exceptions as 'ways in which people recover experiences at odds with their dominant story. By highlighting different events, they are opening space for the authoring of new stories' (p. 296). If exceptions can be identified and owned by the client, replicating or expanding them can become an integral part of their strategy. Gilligan and Price (1993) describe the process of working with exceptions as 'deviation amplifying feedback' (p. 104). There are always variations in the way people experience and handle stress, although it may feel to them as if it is rigid and pervasive. In fact if they could watch themselves on video they would see that there are occasions when their stress level goes down and even recedes into the background as other thoughts, feelings and behaviours come to the foreground. There are times when the symptoms of stress/anxiety/depression appear but are somehow curtailed or short circuited and there are times when they go away altogether for a period of time. The length of intervals between episodes may vary. One of the consequences of high levels of stress is that the sufferer loses a sense of perspective and proportion – to such an extent that everything is a problem and they fail to distinguish between a major crisis and the 'small stuff'. At such times everything becomes a source of stress, even activities which they normally enjoy. This loss of perspective ('not seeing the wood for the trees') and being on constant alert for perceived danger means that the client is unlikely to notice those times when he or she is not stressed. Exceptions provide new data which could potentially widen the client's awareness, not only of times when the problem is absent but also of times when they are doing other things instead. At exceptional times the client is recovering the kind of life they want – a life without the problem or at least with it cut down to size.

The solution-focused counsellor listens for and enquires about possible exceptions to the problem. Exceptions are times when the problem (a) is temporarily absent, (b) is present but does not affect the client as much as usual, (c) does not last as long or is not experienced as intensely or (d) does not happen with the same frequency. Clients report exceptions when they recall pre-session changes; when they discover exceptions during the problem exploration phase and when they become aware of exceptions during the discussion of the miracle question. Exceptions are small miracles. When the client provides examples of exceptions they may also proffer explanations as to why they took place. This can be either helpful or unhelpful. It can be unhelpful if it fosters explanations which make future exceptions less likely. A detailed description of how the exception came about is as important as the client's speculation about its causes. As Sir Arthur Conan Doyle had Sherlock Holmes say, 'It is a capital mistake to theorize before you have all the evidence. It biases judgement'.

Examples of exceptions would be when there are reports that:

- the client did not lose her temper in circumstances when she usually did
- the client managed to contribute to a meeting at which she was normally silent
- the client was able to talk about the problem without crying
- the client was able to stop thinking about stressful events and think of something else
- the client took a slower pace instead of rushing around out of control
- the client listened to her partner
- the client did not take work home with her for a change.

All of these events were different from the client's normal stress response. The client had done something different. Exceptions can be in the realm of thoughts, feelings or behaviours and usually involve all three. An exception could be to take time out to think about something or to explore the meaning of a new feeling.

The questions which elicit exceptions are invitations to clients to change their vocabulary about their problems. By no means all clients are able to join in this linguistic game. Many cannot initially identify exceptions. Later in the session they often speak of an incident which constitutes an exception, for example, the client was managing her stress level better. Phrases which the client uses can often lead to the discovery of exceptions:

- most of the time
- quite often
- normally
- just for a change
- hardly ever
- occasionally
- from time to time
- sometimes
- rarely
- once in a while.

Then the counsellor asks the client directly: 'Have there been any times recently when the stress/anxiety/depression was not so bad or you felt you were handling it better?' Alternatively, the counsellor may refer back to one of the above phrases, 'You said earlier that most of the time you felt overwhelmed and out of control. Has there been a time when you felt even some control over events?' 'Normally you said you would have three glasses of wine one after the other as soon as you got home. Do you ever find that you do not have three glasses or maybe even none at all?' For clients who find it difficult to believe that improvement is possible, the counsellor will ask questions about the different degrees of severity in the problem, for example, 'Have there been any times, *even when you were still feeling depressed*, when it was not as bad as at other times?'

If the client is able to report an exception then the counsellor follows it up with questions such as, 'Could you tell me more about how that came about? Where were you? Who were you with? What were you doing/saying/thinking/feeling? Did it make a difference to you or to anyone else? How did you manage to do/not do it? What happened after this happened? Is this something you would be interested in making happen again?'

Implicit in these questions is the message that the client had some degree of control and choice over the exception. Often the counsellor will compliment the client for their part in making these exceptions happen. This may influence the client to reappraise exceptions as being more important than they originally thought. These incidents provide rich and fertile soil for discovering the client's unique way of dealing with problems. Exceptions may be either planned or spontaneous.

Planned exceptions

These are courses of action which the client deliberately initiates in order to change the problem situation. The more planned exceptions the client can recall the closer she is to having an effective strategy. When the client explores with the counsellor the exception or exceptions to the problem, it is for the purpose of increasing her awareness of thought processes, feelings and actions around the exception. The sequence of interactions with others is examined. Recognizing that she used her own power to create the exceptions is in itself empowering. Heightened awareness of exceptions also contributes to self-fulfilling prophecies. The more she looks for exceptions the more she is likely to create them. The counsellor will encourage her to keep doing what is already working and to look for further opportunities to extend her planned exceptions.

EXAMPLE

Client: I feel that the work I do is never recognized. No one ever thanks me or praises me. They think that if they give us the occasional bonus that is enough to motivate us, but that does not work for me. I would prefer if they told you when you had done a good piece of work.

Counsellor: How do you handle this lack of recognition?

Client: It might sound pathetic but I make a point of telling my manager when I have done something good. I do not think he listens but at least I feel I have made a point.

Counsellor: Does that make a difference for you?

Client: Yes. I know in this job I have to rely on myself. It is important for me not to be down on myself and only notice mistakes. It helps to celebrate when I know I did well. I have one colleague with whom I go out for lunch and we encourage each other.

Counsellor: I know you would like to get recognition from the management but it sounds important for you to recognize what you do well and to find someone else to acknowledge it as well. It helps you to keep a sense of achievement about your work.

Spontaneous exceptions

These are exceptions which happen apparently by chance without any planning or conscious action by the client. Clients tend to be mystified by such occurrences and are unable to identify what made the difference. They may put the exception down to some external factor beyond their control (luck or fate) or to something which only happens very rarely or is not replicable. They may feel that the circumstances surrounding the exception render it invalid in terms of problem resolution. For example, they feel relaxed and happy when off work but they do not see how this can help them face the demands of the workplace. Some exceptions are attributed to actions which are in themselves problematic: 'I was okay when I was drinking', 'I don't have panic attacks as long as I stay in the house'. Such exceptions are not helpful. They are failed solutions which have become part of the problem. Some exceptions are worse than the problem. The counsellor explores the spontaneous exceptions with the client to discover whether some aspect of the experience is within the client's control. The counsellor helps the client to find ways in which a spontaneous exception could be translated into a planned exception. For example, there may be elements of the holiday which could be continued in some form when the client returns to her normal routine. She may realize that she needs more rest, more time on her own or more fun.

If clients can only find spontaneous exceptions they will be given the task of looking for planned exceptions. Finding exceptions helps to break down the client's rigid definition of the problem and opens up possibilities for change. Clients may be invited to keep an exception diary in which they record exceptions to the problem. The following excerpts are from a client's exception diary.

Exception diary
(Client suffers from chronic anxiety. Exceptions are in italics.)

Monday
Always a bad day. Feel very wound up. Dreading going to work. Feel very panicky as I travel to work. Feel urge to turn round and go home. *Listen to some music on my walkman and it calms me down.* Get into work – feeling worried about the staff meeting as I am chairing it. *Talk to Steve who makes me laugh, feel less stressed.* Instead of staying at my desk at lunch time *I went for a ten minute walk around the shops, not exactly beautiful, but at least it was a break.*

Tuesday
Found myself dwelling on all the things that are going wrong in my life. Feeling quite depressed. *Sent a few e-mails to some friends and had a moan, cheered me up a bit.*
This afternoon I felt really restless. When I am doing something I always think I should be doing something else but not sure what. *Talked to myself about it and made myself concentrate on one thing at a time.*

Wednesday
Had panic attack at home for no apparent reason, just hit me out of the blue when I

was watching television. No idea why it should happen. Normally lasts for about fifteen or twenty minutes but *I practised my breathing and relaxation exercises and found that it began to subside after five or six minutes.* I felt quite pleased that I had handled it better than I normally do.

White (1989) describes exceptions as 'unique outcomes which contradict aspects of the problem-saturated description' the client brings. Discovering exceptions generates an alternative narrative for the client, one which is more balanced and open to change. White describes three stages in developing exceptions with the client:

(1) Place the unique outcome within the context of some pattern of events by using questions such as: How did you know what to do in that situation? How did you set it up? Does this fit with anything else that's been happening recently? (2) Ascribe meaning to them: What does this tell you about yourself or other people? How does that affect the way you see yourself now? What does it mean for you when she does that? (3) Speculate about new possibilities arising from these new descriptions: What difference will it make for you now that you have done that? What do you think the next step for you is? How will you know it is a good time to take it?   (White, 1989: 41–5)

White provides a wide range of direct and indirect questions which the counsellor can use to build upon reported exceptions.

Miller sums up the role of exception seeking in the rewriting of clients' stories:

Constructing solutions is not about making up fictional stories about clients' lives, but about creating stories that make it possible for clients to see and learn from what is already there. The new stories make it possible for clients to learn from their own successes, and for therapists to better utilise clients' abilities and resources in helping them solve their problems.   (Miller, 1997: 197)

Armstrong (1999) suggests a variation on exception questions which he calls 'nearly, almost did it' type questions. These are times when the client almost managed to do what she was trying to do. Although the client may in a sense have failed, the conversation pays more attention to 'what it was that she learned from this event and also what would need to happen to take things a step further the next time' (p. 17). If there are specific circumstances which limit the client's current choices, for example, lack of money, the exception-seeking question may include the following. 'Can you think of a time when you were happy even though you had no money?' (Conlon, 2000).

UTILIZATION OF CLIENT STRENGTHS

The counsellor sets out to help the client to reconnect with their resources, strengths and qualities which she needs to solve the problem (de Shazer, 1988a). As well as identifying the resources it is helpful if the client can remember *how* she deployed them in the past. Armed with that knowledge she may become aware of how to reactivate them in the present. Her current problem may of course differ from those in the past but there could be a discernible pattern of coping and non-coping behaviour. The counsellor asks questions to elicit the client's coping skills.

COPING QUESTIONS

- How did you get through that?
- What helped you at the time?
- What were you thinking/saying to yourself?
- What did anyone else say/do?
- What did you find was not useful for you?
- What did that situation mean for you?
- What do you need to remember next time you feel you are not coping?

EXAMPLE

A client who had felt suicidal after the death of her mother experienced similar thoughts and feelings on the breakdown of her marriage. With the counsellor she recalled how she had coped with her grief. She was able to explore how she could use those resources again.

We know that many people with psychological problems are 'spontaneous improvers' and that most people do not have recourse to professional help when they experience problems in life. They adapt to the problems which their environment creates by using their skills, beliefs, positive personal qualities and social networks. In solution-focused work the counsellor brings those resources into the client's awareness. This does not mean clients possess fully formed solutions within themselves. The counsellor believes the client has resources which are not being fully employed in resolving her problem. It is the task of the counsellor to help clients own and apply their resources or to extend or modify their existing repertoire of life skills.

A straw poll of people on a workshop revealed the following list of skills, values and strategies which helped them when they were stressed:

- Ensuring I had some rewards or treats
- Prioritizing the problems
- Using my sense of humour
- Recognizing the signs of stress in time
- Having a long-term project or goal
- To be heard by someone who really listened and understood
- Having outlets to re-create myself
- Hobbies and interests
- Being disciplined
- Getting out of the house
- Finding some time to be on my own
- Sleeping
- Taking one day at a time

- Asking for different kinds of help from different people
- Learning to say 'no' to demands.

The list identifies a range of personal skills, for example, to be assertive, to manage time and to be intimate. It names personal qualities, for example, self-discipline or a sense of humour. Underlying these strengths there is a personal sense of value – 'I have the right to say no to the demands of others, I have a right to my own space'. Without a sense of self-respect the client is unlikely to own personal strengths and resources. In times of stress people can lose sight of their own inherent self-worth. Their vulnerability may allow others to deny them their rights as a person. The emphasis on the rights of the individual is more in keeping with western culture so for a client from a different culture the list of solutions may be different. For example, a strength may be the network of mutual obligations which bind members of a community together. In some situations this can equally be a source of stress.

THE MIRACLE QUESTION

The question, devised by Steve de Shazer (1988a), has a standard formula:

> Imagine when you go to sleep one night a miracle happens and the problems which we've been talking about disappear. As you were asleep, you did not know that a miracle had happened. When you woke up what would be the first signs for you that a miracle had happened?

This is a central intervention in the solution-focused approach. It is used in the first and in subsequent sessions. The counsellor uses this question to help clients describe their goals, resources, exceptions and strategies. It is a hypothetical question which invites them to imagine and describe in some detail what life will be like when they no longer have the problem(s). It is not really about miracles at all (in my view the term itself is not helpful).

In asking the miracle question the counsellor makes an assumption that some of the 'miracle' is in fact already happening and all the client needs to do is to locate these changes and amplify them. These 'small miracles' (exceptions) have been submerged under a sea of problems. The timing of the question is important as clients will be unwilling to engage in the kind of thinking required to answer it until they feel that the counsellor has heard and understood their problem. It can be asked at any stage of the process but is often introduced after the client has engaged in as much problem talk as is necessary. In most cases it will be asked during the first session. The question enables the counsellor to explore the client's preferred future without further reference to the presenting problem. This is in keeping with the fundamental tenet of the solution-focused approach that solutions are differentiated from the problems. Miller (1997) states, 'Problem definition becomes superfluous once clients have specified the details of their miracles' (p. 81). The miracle question is useful when the client is vague about her problem and the counsellor is finding it difficult to understand what her concerns are. Paradoxically, it can happen that by exploring the preferred future the nature of the problem also becomes clearer. Over the course of a number of sessions the miracle question may be asked more than once. The answer often changes as the client changes.

The miracle question is asked slowly with pauses between the phrases to allow the client to engage with the picture which it generates. Some clients report the experience as being almost trancelike. If it feels appropriate, the counsellor may encourage the client to enter further into the miracle scenario by visualizing what he would see/taste/hear/touch/smell. Some clients may even be able to dramatize 'the morning after the miracle' with the counsellor.

The miracle question helps clients to clarify their goals and the means to achieve them. It encourages them to articulate in concrete terms those experiences which they would like to have in their lives and then invites them to consider how they could make them come about. The answer to the miracle question also brings to light past and current mini-solutions and available resources. Of course the miracle question does not require clients to believe in miracles. Some clients may find the religious overtones of the term *miracle* difficult or find the concept unhelpful in which case it can be asked in a different form, for example:

Imagine you were on holiday and when you came back somehow things had been sorted out, how would you know? What would be the first signs for you that something amazing had happened?

Other alternatives might include variations on the following:

- Suppose you were starting this job/relationship again, what things would you like to be different?
- If you were aiming to bring about changes in this area of your life, what would be the first signs for you that you were making progress?

The miracle question is an imaginative and creative device which, although apparently simple and even banal, often succeeds in generating from the client a rich narrative of life without the problem. It cuts through the dead wood of linear thinking with its accompanying rationalizations and denials and releases new life into moribund conversations. In bringing the future into clear focus it empowers the client to act constructively in the present. It has similarities with the behavioural techniques of forward chaining – where the counsellor takes the client through the sequence of actions required to get to a desired end-point – and to back chaining – where the counsellor starts with the desired end result, for example, going out to the shops, and works back to retrace what the steps were that helped the client to do it. In exploring the miracle question the counsellor often blurs time boundaries so that at one moment the counsellor is talking about the future/past, 'How did you control your panic attacks?' (in the miracle). The counsellor then moves into the present/past, 'Are there times when you control your panic attacks at the moment?' (exceptions). Then into the present/future, 'So how are you thinking you will control your panic attacks?'

The hypothetical nature of the miracle question allows clients to rise above self-defeating restrictive thinking. It encourages clients to escape temporarily from their preoccupation with their problems and to divert their thinking and imagination into solution construction. It gives reality to other perspectives and recruits the client into a new way of seeing their situation. However, it is not helpful to allow the client to develop the answer to the miracle question in such a way that she feels even more despondent and powerless about the gap between the ideal and her reality. Answering the miracle question is not easy for many clients, particularly if they have had multiple chronic problems, few memorable good times and little sense of self-agency. Their negative predictions about life make it hard to entertain the possibility that the future could be different from the present and the past. Their cautious or underdeveloped imagination and low sense of self-esteem will have contributed to the entrenching of their problem. Their experience of failure and the low expectations of those around them will have reinforced their internalized belief that they do not have a right to anything better than that which they have. The dominant culture may have socialized the individual into this position by stigmatizing and discriminating against her. The client and the counsellor are not detached from this social context and will be influenced by the prevailing norms. As well as holding a negative and pessimistic mindset, the client may also have a mixture of negative feelings about herself and the world around her. She may feel defeated, confused and scared. The client may wish these feelings and thoughts would go away but have no clear sense of how different her life could be. She may believe that it really would take a miracle for her situation to improve. This belief makes her feel even more powerless. Counsellors need to work slowly and patiently with such clients, giving them time and space to see the world through a very different pair of spectacles.

EXAMPLE

Counsellor: I would like to ask you a strange question but one which many people find helpful.
(*This preamble catches the imagination of the client. It suggests that although it may sound an odd question, the effort required to answer it will bring some benefits.*)

Counsellor: Imagine that when you go to sleep tonight a miracle happens and all of the difficulties which you have been having disappear. Because you are asleep, you don't know that a miracle has happened. When you wake up in the morning what will be the first signs for you that a miracle has happened?

Client: I don't know.
(*This initial response is common. The counsellor needs to be silent and let the client enter into the spirit of the question. As in most forms of therapies, there are moments when the counsellor has to stay calm and wait for something to happen. If the client cannot get started the counsellor will ask supplementary questions to encourage the client.*)

Counsellor: So what would you be seeing when ...?

Client: I would feel as if I had got my life back.

Counsellor: How would you know? What would be the first sign for you that you were starting to get your life back?

Client: My partner and I would be sleeping in the same bed for a start.

Counsellor: That has not been happening for a while?

Client: We decided a while ago that I should sleep in the spare bed because I was always coming to bed late and wakening her up. I was wakening her up during the night as well, because I was tossing and turning in my sleep. I would wake up early and not be able to get back to sleep and then I would wake her up again. We were both exhausted and bad tempered in the morning so we decided that for a while I should sleep next door.

Counsellor: So after the miracle what would be happening?

Client: I would be getting a decent night's sleep and we would be back together in bed.

Counsellor: What would the first thing that would need to happen to give you a chance of a better night's sleep?

Client: I've thought about not working at home so much at night. When I go to bed my head's still full of problems and worries.

Counsellor: So after the miracle you would be working less in the evening – not right until you go to bed – and you would have found ways of drawing a line under the day. What sort of things would you have done?

Client: I would spend some time with my partner before she goes to bed, maybe just watch television together. I think I am withdrawing from everyone because I feel so stressed. My partner is fed up with it and we have had rows about it.

Counsellor: So after the miracle you would finish work earlier and spend more time with your partner in the evening. What else?

The phrase 'what else?' figures highly in a solution-focused counsellor's vocabulary. It is employed to elicit detailed answers to different types of questions.

Clients may want to explore a range of answers to the miracle question. For example, what the miracle would look like if they stayed in a job or what it would look like if they left. When clients inevitably depart from the miracle script and return to problem talk the counsellor brings them back on to the solution track while validating their concerns.

Counsellor: It sounds as if both you and your partner are convinced of the need to change the balance of things. What else would you notice that was different after the miracle?

When clients find it difficult to answer the miracle question because they can only see problems, the counsellor reminds them that in this conversation the miracle has actually happened, so the difficulty or problem they are raising has been overcome.

It is important for the counsellor to use interpersonal skills such as active listening, paraphrasing, summarizing and empathy to help clients expand their 'miracle' scenarios. Even when clients create unrealistic scenarios the counsellor can still use them, either by scaling down the miracle –'it's not as big as that'– or by extracting the attainable elements from the picture. It becomes apparent that the client does not need a miracle to make some of her 'miracle' come true.

The detailed exploration of the answer to the miracle question leads to the unearthing of exceptions to the problems, the clarification of small goals, the generation of potential strategies and the identification of personal strengths and skills. The dialogue between the counsellor and the client becomes an interweaving of these solution themes. The information elicited in the process will become the centre piece of the feedback which the counsellor gives to the client at the end of each session.

Having identified a raft of desired changes, the counsellor then asks a range of relationship questions which locate the client in her social network and draw out from her the positive benefits which could result from making some of this miracle become a reality. These relationship questions tend to follow a circular pattern (Burnham, 1986):

- So if your partner began to do that how would that affect you?
- If, after the miracle, you were less stressed and getting on better with your partner how would the children notice?
- If you were happier at home who at work would notice what was different about you?
- What would you notice was different about other people in your life?
- What do you think your partner would say if she could hear your answer to the miracle question?
- What do you think would be her answer to the miracle question?

During the discussion of the miracle answer the counsellor finds out which strategies may help to bring about the desired changes. Since the client is talking hypothetically she is likely to be less defensive. The counsellor is listening out for reports of current successful strategies which the client could develop further. In the first instance the counsellor tries to discover whether any existing strategies are working. If they are working, the client might be interested in finding out how to maintain or even extend them. If they are not working, she might be willing to discard them and do something different. When the client feels that nothing is working and they have tried everything, the counsellor needs to be supportive and empathic and not pressurize the client into being more optimistic. With the belief that the client is cooperating as best she can, the counsellor will not force the pace but move at the client's tempo.

Clients often become animated and energetic when answering the miracle question. Solution talk also seems to encourage a humour in which both parties enjoy laughing at some aspects of the situation. Publicly expressing their hopes in the miracle answer can in itself help to motivate clients towards their goals. Clients often report how surprised they were by their answers to the miracle question.

The counsellor helps the client to further develop their answers to the miracle question by active listening, prompting, empathizing and therapeutic questioning. The counsellor does this by:

- Inviting the client to describe in detail the day after the miracle and by exploring how the differences in one part of the day will affect the rest of the day.

Counsellor: So when things go much better at work, what will it be like when you come home in the evening?

Counsellor: When you manage to handle the children better during the day, what will be happening in the evening?

- Asking questions about other significant people and how the miracle would affect them.

Counsellor: Who will be the first person in the family to notice a miracle has happened? How will they react?
Counsellor: What difference will that make to you?
Counsellor: How will you know that they have found out?
Counsellor: How will your partner behave now that the miracle has happened?

- Focusing on feelings as well as behaviour.

Counsellor: How will you feel if you manage to do that?

Is it always appropriate to use the miracle question? Some practitioners advocate caution when using it in situations where it could be construed as insensitive, for example, when the client has a terminal illness or has suffered a recent bereavement. These are situations when the most likely answer to the miracle question is something unattainable, such as a bereaved person wanting the return of the person who has died. Some counsellors would customize the question to rule out this answer which they feel would be unhelpful for the client. Others prefer to 'work with what you've got' and argue that much helpful information can come from the question, even in these circumstances. De Shazer (1998b, p. 2) argues that the miracle question can usefully be asked even when, or in fact particularly when, he anticipates a not so useful response.

In my own practice, I tend to ask a modified form of the miracle question in similar circumstances. Possible alternative versions might be:

- If you were aiming to bring about change in this area of your life, what would be the first signs that you were making progress?
- If you came into work tomorrow (went to school, were at home or wherever the problem takes place) and the problems which are bothering you were solved, how would you notice?
- Suppose you were starting (your job, this relationship) again, and it was much more like the way you would like it to be, how would it look? What would there be more or less of?

Much of what the client reveals in the answers to the miracle question are the client's goals. The counsellor explores with the client the last time when she experienced even one small part of the miracle. If the client is able to describe such an event it becomes an exception to the problem which could possibly be expanded. Santa Rita Jr (1998) suggests that, particularly with clients who have ill-defined goals or problems, it can be helpful to encourage clients to simplify their response to the miracle question. This is done by encouraging the client to focus closely upon the smallest piece of the miracle which is achievable and which will signal to the client that she is moving in the right direction. This micro step need not be related directly to the presenting problem but progress in one area may lead to progress throughout the system.

On the rare occasion when a person is unable or possibly unwilling to respond to the miracle question, the counsellor may ask a series of time projection questions such as:

- If I were to meet you in three/six months time and you were telling me things were better than they are now, what would you tell me you or anyone else did to make it happen?
- What would have been the first thing that happened and what would have happened after that?

The miracle question asks a lot from a client and not everyone is able to enter into the spirit of it but when they do it can become a rich mine for developing alternative scenarios for change. On a practical note it is difficult to remember answers to the miracle question without taking notes at the time. The counsellor will need to refer to this information when it is time for giving the client feedback. Taking notes also reinforces the importance of these steps towards finding solutions.

CHAPTER 5

Second Steps

SCALING

Solution-focused counsellors use a technique called scaling (de Shazer and Berg, 1992). This technique helps clients to express their thoughts and feelings about their problem through the use of numbers. The scale ranges from 0–10, with 0 representing the worst the problem has ever been, or what it was like prior to the client requesting counselling, and 10 representing there no longer being a problem. However the client answers the scaling questions the counsellor works with the relationship between the numbers (de Shazer, 1994). This is applicable whether the scales relate to progress, confidence, motivation or any other aspect of the client's situation. If the client says he is 3 on the scale it implies he is at least one-third of the way to solving his problem. Clients rarely entertain the ambition of reaching 10.

Scales often generate hope where previously the client felt none and we know that hopefulness is an important ingredient in effective outcomes (Miller *et al.*, 1997). Using numbers to rate the problem pins it down more. Whether the client rates himself as moving up or down the scale the counsellor will ask questions about the movement between the numbers. This elicits answers about exceptions, successful strategies, coping mechanisms, goal definition and first small steps to be taken.

Scaling may be used at any point in the sessions, depending upon the judgement of the counsellor. Typically, however, it is used in first sessions following the exploration of the miracle question. It is also used as an opening intervention in second and remaining sessions. Scaling will often relate to specific goals and strategies which have emerged from the answer to the miracle question. Scaling brings the miraculous down to earth.

Scaling:

- engages clients as active participants
- gives clients the power to evaluate their own situations
- communicates to clients they have some control and choice over their problem

- draws out concrete illustrations of clients' resources and competence
- elicits graphic descriptions of goals and the small steps to take towards them
- identifies exceptions (how they moved up the scale)
- enables clients to identify and evaluate signs of progress
- gives clients a tool which they can use themselves between sessions and at the end of counselling
- helps clients to link solutions in one area of their lives to other areas
- builds confidence, hope and motivation.

In the experience of most counsellors, scaling is an accessible and helpful tool for clients, irrespective of their problem. It is empowering for clients to have their ratings respected and accepted by the counsellor. It illustrates to clients that their views and ideas are more relevant and important than those of the counsellors. This may be particularly important for the client whose confidence and self-esteem are low because of the stress which they are experiencing. At times the counsellor may be tempted to challenge clients about their self-rating, for example, when the counsellor feels that a client is not giving himself enough credit for progress which has been made. Rather than challenge the scale it is usually more productive and conducive to cooperation to accept the client's judgement. Using scales to measure progress and to see how to take small steps forward can be helpful to someone who feels life is out of control. By the counsellor accepting and supporting the client's self-rating a sense of partnership is created between them. In describing himself as a 4 or 5, the client is attaching a significance to the number. There is a danger the counsellor could assume she knows what the numbers represent, for example, if the client describes himself as a 2 or 3 the counsellor may imagine this represents a low rating whereas in the client's eyes this might be quite a high score. As de Shazer (1994) puts it, 'Scaling questions allow both therapist and client to jointly construct a bridge, a way of talking about things that are hard to describe' (p. 92).

Sometimes the answers clients give to scaling questions can surprise the counsellor. The client may present a complex problem, but see himself as a 5, while the counsellor was anticipating a rating of 1 or 2. Scaling keeps the counsellor close to the client! De Shazer and his colleagues (de Shazer and Berg, 1992) began to use scaling in their work. They found that clients could use it to express what he meant, even if the meaning was not clear to anyone else. As long as the client knew what he meant when he moved up and down the scale, that was all that mattered.

The following is an excerpt from a first interview with a client who is trying to recover from a violent incident at work.

Client: I still feel very frightened when I open up the office in the morning, especially in these dark winter mornings.

Counsellor: On a scale of 0–10, with 10 being you feel safe and recovered from the attack and 0 being you still feel in danger, where do you feel you are at the moment?

Client: About a 4, but some days I am at square one. If you had asked me last week when I phoned you I would have said 1.

Here the client is making a number of points:

- my sense of safety fluctuates
- I have been worse
- something helpful has happened since I contacted you.

Counsellor: How did you move from 1 to 4?

Client: Ever since this happened we have been supporting each other at work. If anyone feels a bit down someone else takes them off for a coffee. Since we were all involved we understand if someone has a bad day and bursts into tears for no apparent reason.

Counsellor: So getting support at work helps? What else got you to a 4?

Client: Well, management were very slow to start with. They seemed to be more concerned about the insurance policy than with the staff. Our regional manager was useless, he did not know what to say. But now they have improved the security in the shop, it could not happen the same way again. We all felt better after that.

Counsellor: Did it mean a lot to the staff that they did that?

Client: Yes, it did.

Counsellor: What else keeps you at 4?

This question represents a shift from how the client reached 4, to how she maintains being a 4.

Client: My parents have been great. If I ever want to talk about it my Mum always listens. I am trying to get back to normal and just get on with it. My Dad said, 'Don't let it ruin your life. Get back to normal.' I went out with some friends for a drink the other night, that is the first time I've done that since the attack.

Counsellor: How did you manage to do that?

Client: They have been asking me for ages but I have always said no. But my boyfriend said he would pick me up and bring me back. He said if I only wanted to stay for an hour or so, that would be all right.

Counsellor: Would staying at 4 for a while be all right or are you thinking it is time to move to a 5?

Client: I don't know. I don't want any pressure, I want to do it my way.

Counsellor: Sure.

Client: I think once we get the trial out of the way, that will really help.

Counsellor: How is that? What will that mean to you?

Client: Hopefully, they will go down, then I will feel safer. The police say they could get three to five years.

Counsellor: Right.

In the following scenario we can see how scaling can help clients to clarify where they would like to get to and how they might get there.

Counsellor: So you are off work at the moment and that seems to help in reducing your stress level. On a scale of 0–10 with 10 being you are back to the way you were before you had this problem, where do you feel you are today?

Client:	2.
Counsellor:	What helps you to avoid being a 1?
Client:	My friends.
Counsellor:	How do they help?
Client:	They keep me in touch with what is happening at work. They still invite me when they go out. They come round to the house and take me out of myself.
Counsellor:	So you are a 2 at the moment and your friends keep you going, sounds as if they're a good bunch of friends.
Client:	They are great, they would do anything for me.
Counsellor:	On the scale of 0–10, where would you need to get to before you felt it was the right time to go back to work?
Client:	I wish I could get another job.
Counsellor:	Is that something you're thinking about?
Client:	It is not practical at the moment. You can't apply for a job when you have been off sick for nearly three months.
Counsellor:	So at the moment, going back seems like your only choice?
Client:	Yes.
Counsellor:	So when you know 'now is the right time to go back' – because you don't want to go back and be off sick again – where will you be on the scale?
Client:	7.
Counsellor:	How will you know you are a 7, what will be happening?
Client:	I would have sorted something out with my manager. I would feel better in myself. I'd have gone back to visit before I go back for good.
Counsellor:	Right. So after the visit what would you hope would be different which would get you to a 7?
Client:	I would know that I could handle it. I would work out ways of getting out of the office more and meeting clients, which is the bit of the job I enjoy. I'd be off the medication because I know it makes me sleepy and I can't concentrate. I would have to be off it for a couple of weeks before I would go back.
Counsellor:	What else would let you know it was time to go back?
Client:	I would listen to my partner's advice because he knows me best. If he didn't think I was ready he would tell me.
Counsellor:	So you would be a 7 and ready to go back to work when you were off the medication, had visited work, had a plan and your partner agreed you were ready. What do you see happening over the next few weeks?
Client:	I don't think much is going to happen in the run-up to Christmas. Going back then would be a bad idea. Lots of people would be off and there would be lots of pressure for those on duty. I would wait till the New Year. I am hoping that I can get off the tablets before Christmas. I could visit the office then too, so I might go back to work in mid-January.

The above excerpt demonstrates how the approach not only helps clients to observe change but also helps them to imagine it (Miller, 1997). As well as eliciting the client's own self-rating or scales, the client can be invited to imagine how other people who know him would scale him. Whether the answer is higher or lower on the scale, it can be used to draw out what the client is doing already that is helpful.

In the following example the client is in conflict with her boss.

Counsellor: You feel you are a 4 at the moment and you would like to be a 7. If your colleague/partner/friend/parent were here at the moment, where would they say you were on the scale?

Client: My friends would say I am about a 5 or 6.

Counsellor: What do they know about you which makes them describe you as a 6?

Client: They think that I am really good at standing up for myself but I feel I'm a complete wimp.

Counsellor: What is their evidence for this? What have they seen you doing?

Client: Some of them are scared stiff to take things back to a shop. They always want me to go with them. They often ask me to do the talking because I can sound firm without losing my temper.

Counsellor: That sounds like a useful skill, lots of people find that difficult. How do you do it?

Client: Well I just think I had to work hard to buy that and if it is no good, I've done all that work for nothing and why should I get ripped off?

Counsellor: How do you manage to sound strong and give off the 'you're not messing with me' message without losing your temper when they try to brush you off?

Client: I stand near other customers and speak quite loudly without shouting. I find they want you to shut up in case you put other customers off buying things.

Counsellor: Sounds like a clever tactic. Where did you learn that?

Client: My mother used to do that and it always worked. I guess I learned from watching her. She never let people take advantage of her but she was always polite about it. It now works for me.

If the client were to say that other people, for example, her boss, rated her lower than she rated herself, the counsellor may ask:

Counsellor: You feel that despite all the stress you are an 8. What would your boss say?

Client: Probably a 3 or 4.

Counsellor: How come?

Client: He has no idea what our work is like. He only sees what he wants to see. People tell him what they think he wants to hear. He is always there when things go wrong but he never says anything good when things are going well.

Counsellor: What does he not know about you which would make him realize you are an 8 not a 4?

Client: It would help if he understood the level of abuse we receive from the general public. We have to bite our tongues. He does not know what it is like to be threatened by someone who is angry because they think we are cheating them. I would like to see him cope with it.

Counsellor: So he does not know how difficult the job is and what it takes to do it. Is there anything in particular he does not know about you?

Client: He does not know how I have to juggle looking after my children and doing the job. I would like to see him do a day's work, dash home, collect the kids from the childminder, get them home, feed them, put them to bed, tidy the house and then start to make a meal for myself. I am exhausted. He does not know what it's like trying to take time off to look after your kids when they are sick. He has an easy life.

Counsellors use scales to help clients (a) assess the current state of the problem and (b) gauge their level of confidence at solving the problem.

EXAMPLE

Counsellor: On a scale of 0–10, with 10 being you are absolutely confident that you can deal with this problem and 0 being you would like to but you have no confidence, where would you put yourself today?

Client: About a 7.

Counsellor: What makes you say 7?

Client: I have done harder things. I know when I make up my mind no one can stop me.

Counsellor: You can be determined about something you really want.

Client: I do not give up easily. No one gives you anything for nothing. You have to make things happen. No one else will do it for me.

Counsellor: So is a 7 good enough to begin to make a start?

Client: I think so.

Counsellor: What will be the first step that lets you know you are on your way?

Counsellors also use scales to elicit commitment from clients. Scaling can help to identify how much the client is willing to invest in making changes.

EXAMPLE

Counsellor: On a scale of 0–10 with 10 being you would do anything to control your anger and 0 being you do not think you will be able to do much, where would you put yourself today?

Client: 6.

Counsellor: Is that high enough for you to make a start?

Client: It will have to be. If I do not start to make changes my partner is going to end our relationship.

Counsellor: And you want this relationship to continue?

Client: Yes. I do not want to lose everything we have built up. I do not want to lose contact with my daughter.

Counsellor: What makes you feel that 6 will be enough?

Client: It has made me come here for a start. I have had a good talk with my partner and I have apologized for losing my temper.

Counsellor: Does your partner know that you are a 6 in terms of making changes?

Client: I don't know if she trusts me yet. I don't blame her. I think she feels she has heard it all before. She wants actions not words.

Counsellor: How would she rate how serious you are this time in sorting it out?

Client: I think she would probably say a 3.

Counsellor: What is it about you at the moment that she finds it hard to see? What would

	convince her that you really were a 6 this time and that this was going to be a turning point for both of you?
Client:	She would say, stop talking about it and just do it.
Counsellor:	Do what exactly?
Client:	Cut down on the drinking ... Spend more time with her ... Do some jobs about the house.
Client:	Which of those do you think she needs to see first?
Counsellor:	If I were to come home earlier, then she would know I was serious about cutting down on the drinking.
Counsellor:	Is that where you would start or would you start somewhere else?
Client:	I have already started. I came home early on two occasions last week.
Counsellor:	Did that make a difference for you both?
Client:	Yes it was okay. There were no arguments anyway.
Counsellor:	What would you need to keep you at a 6 next week?
Client:	I need to get fit again. I am out of condition.
Counsellor:	Are you thinking of doing something about that?
Client:	I need to go to the gym again.

Palmer's technique of stress mapping (1990) uses a similar scale. Stress mapping is a visual technique which helps the counsellor and the client to identify the source of interpersonal and environmental stressors. The client is viewed as part of an interactional sytem. A diagram is drawn which represents different aspects and relationships in the client's life. Each aspect or relationship is scaled in terms of the degree of stress it contributes to the client's life. The counsellor then explores with the client the systemic nature of the stressors. Having identified and understood these the counsellor can help the client to develop strategies for reducing or eliminating them.

In the diagram we can see that new technology is an important stressor for Karen. Her feelings of inadequacy in using the new computer network are causing her a great deal of anxiety. To reduce the stress level from 8 to 6 she decided she would:

- ask a sympathetic colleague to explain how the new computer system worked
- request training from management
- check she had the correct manual for the machine
- remind herself that it was not her fault that the technology kept breaking down
- find ways to stop thinking about it when she was at home.

A second stressor was her sense of responsibility for her elderly mother. Her mother lived some distance away and was not in good health. Karen worried about her having a fall and being unable to summon assistance. She felt guilty she did not visit her often enough and was worried how she would cope with her guilt if something happened to her mother. She decided she would:

- persuade/pay for her mum to join a local warden scheme in which her day-to-day safety would be monitored
- visit her mum as often as she could and not feel guilty when she couldn't
- pay for a chiropodist and a hairdresser to call each month as her appearance was very important to her mum.

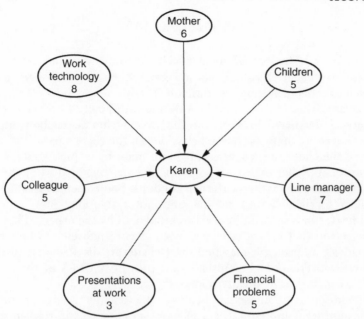

Figure 5.1 *Stress mapping*

Stress is a two-way process. Karen's stress map revealed people who were both the causes of her stress and were affected by it, who as a result further added to her stress levels. Those affected by it in turn may further add to her stress levels. For example, when she is stressed at work she tends to be irritable and critical of her children. This negative behaviour may contribute to her children's poor school performance which, in turn, adds to their stress levels and to her own. Karen is also suffering from stress arising from poor working relationships with a colleague and her line manager. Her line manager is a workaholic who expects his team to work unreasonable hours and carry impossible caseloads. Karen needed to consider how she could be more assertive about this and how she could develop alliances with colleagues to support her. Her relationship with one colleague was particularly abrasive. Karen's current strategy was to avoid this person as much as possible. This seemed to work up to a point but she felt at some stage she would need to take direct action to improve the relationship. She decided she had enough to cope with at the moment and would prefer to leave this issue until a better time. The scaling questions described previously can be used to help the client make decisions about each source of stress. A person's stress map will always be in a state of change as priorities/life events/strategies alter. It needs to be reviewed regularly.

The next intervention we need to consider is that of task giving.

CONSTRUCTING TASKS

A task is a step or a number of steps which the counsellor and client design as homework for the client. Most clients are ambivalent about change, particularly change which sounds daunting or difficult in the short term. If a client has experienced many failures in the past he will find it difficult to believe anything will make a difference. He may be resigned to the *status quo* no matter how unpleasant it is. But even resignation implies coping behaviour on the client's part. The counsellor can encourage the client to recognize and build upon his coping strategies. Clients often expect the counsellor to provide solutions and are frustrated when they feel that the counsellor is not cooperating with their requests. Some clients invest authority in the counsellor especially if they are desperate for a solution. Some cultures hold professional figures in respect and expect to be advised by the expert. They expect to be given advice and they expect to take it when given. Counsellors who resist giving direction or advice on principle may find these clients are dissatisfied with the service and do not return. The skilled counsellor will present feedback of their own ideas, telling them what they have already told you!

The solution-focused counsellor believes the client's strategies for change, provided they are legal and ethical, are of more importance and relevance than any of her own. People tend to act upon their own ideas. Counsellors may tentatively place ideas for change on the table while at the same time acknowledging that they may not fit the client at this moment in time.

The counsellor offers clients a choice from a number of possible tasks without stating their own personal preference. The counsellor provides a rationale for each task including an evaluation of its advantages and disadvantages. Counsellors may adapt a task in response to the client's verbal or non-verbal responses to it. They may, for example, scale down the size of a task if the client does not respond to it enthusiastically or conversely make a task more demanding if the client appears to be under-challenged by it. No counsellor will want to set a client up for failure by designing a task which the client is not ready, willing or able to do. Experience suggests that it is normally better to err on the side of caution in giving the client tasks. It is often wiser to ask too little of the client rather than too much.

The counsellor discusses possible tasks with the client towards the end of the session. Some counsellors take a break to think about the feedback they would like to give the client and to devise the task to be given. Other counsellors deliver the feedback without giving the client the opportunity to respond to it. Others see this as being inconsistent with the collaborative spirit of the model and argue instead for a two-way dialogue at this point in the session. They claim that by participating in the feedback the client develops a greater sense of ownership of it. They suggest that participation at this point increases the likelihood of the client carrying out the task. De Shazer (1998b) speculates that it is possible to predict whether a client will do the task by studying his body language during the discussion of it.

The feedback should be delivered in a clear, simple and concise way. It should use the client's own words or phrases as a means of strengthening rapport. In deciding which task to give, the counsellor will be guided by the following criteria:

- the client's readiness to act
- the degree of willingness on the part of the client to experiment
- availability of social and personal resources
- how it fits the client's values and priorities
- the balance between the gains for the client and the risks to be taken
- the relation of the task to the client's goals
- the congruence between the task and other interventions such as the client's answers to the miracle and scaling questions
- the fit between the curiosity of the client and the task.

There are different types of tasks used by solution-focused counsellors (Hawkes *et al.*, 1998: 49):

- notice tasks
- do something different tasks
- randomized tasks
- pretend tasks
- keep doing what works

Notice Tasks

Notice tasks are given when clients have (a) struggled to identify exceptions to the problem, (b) are unclear in their answers to the miracle question or (c) have few ideas about what they could do to make things better. A notice task is a task which does not put pressure on the client. It does not require him to do anything other than look out for certain things. Clients may be asked to notice:

- what is already working
- what is not working
- times when x (something constructive) happens
- times when someone else does something they find helpful
- times when the expected problem fails to appear or is managed better
- parts of their lives they would like to see continue.

One form of the notice task (de Shazer and Molnar, 1984) known as the Formula First Session Task (FFST), was originally used at the end of the first session.

> Until the next time we meet, I'd like you just to observe what things are happening in your life/family/work that you'd like to see continue then come back and tell me about it. (p. 297)

However, some practitioners now ask the client this question prior to the first meeting. It is one of de Shazer's (1985) 'skeleton key' interventions. The counsellor asks the client to notice what he does *not* feel the need to change – what he wants to keep in his life. This question invites the client to set the parameters of the problem. It highlights the fact that there are areas of his life which are unaffected by his difficulties and which are functioning quite well. The client can deduce from this information that there is more to him than his problem.

The purpose of a notice task is to broaden the client's field of perception to encompass those parts of his life which are exceptions to the problem. He can then begin to identify those parts of his life which he values and would like to develop. If the client can find this type of evidence it breaks the rigid mould which sets the problem in stone. It is evidence that there are stories the client could tell about himself other than ones of failure. In giving this task, the counsellor implies that she believes there is evidence out there waiting to be discovered. Communicating this belief helps to create a self-fulfilling prophecy for the client. Clients tend to find what they are looking for. They interpret information according to the filters which they are currently using.

Do something different tasks

We have seen that 'do something different' is an axiom of the solution-focused approach. The task may not specify exactly what the 'something different' should be. The counsellor may ask the client to think what the something different could be. Sometimes the counsellor will ask the client to do something different and to notice what happens next, for example, notice the effect the doing something different has on other people. This task highlights the client's sense of agency. It emphasizes his ability to break away from sterile, failed solutions and to experiment with new ways of thinking and acting.

Randomized tasks

A randomized task can be useful when the client feels torn between conflicting strategies. Their indecision and inaction may have become part of the problem. A randomized task involves implementing a strategy on a purely arbitrary basis, for example, by tossing a coin or by changing strategies on alternate days. The client can then reflect upon the impact of each strategy. Being persuaded to jump one way or the other without a convincing rationale can help the client to discover which strategy fits their purpose.

Pretend tasks

According to Hawkes *et al.* (1998) a pretend task is one in which the client is invited to act as if the miracle has happened. This can be useful when the client wants to make changes but does not know where to start or when their willingness to experiment is high and their answer to the miracle question has been clear. They will have provided details of the changes they want, for example, 'I will be smiling more, dressing differently, going to different places'. The counsellor asks the client to act out some aspect of his miracle and to notice what difference this makes.

The following client was stressed when he had to attend a meeting he found intimidating.

Client: After the miracle I would look more confident. I would not hide in the corner. I might even say something – ask a question or make a comment.

Counsellor: What else would be different for you after the miracle?

Client:	The people at the meeting would listen to me with respect.
Counsellor:	What would you look and sound like if that was happening?
Client:	I would be smiling more, talking more and I wouldn't feel so nervous.
Counsellor:	Do you think that for the first ten minutes or so of the next meeting you could pretend that they were interested in what you had to say? You could act as if they were? How do you think you could do that?
Client:	I would need to psyche myself up before the meeting.
Counsellor:	How would you do that?
Client:	I would picture myself being with people who respect me.
Counsellor:	What would that look like?
Client:	I would imagine I was at a meeting at our club instead of at work.
Counsellor:	You sound as if you know how to do that. Could you try it for a few minutes at the start of one meeting and see what happens?

Keep doing what works tasks

'If it works keep doing it' is another solution-focused axiom. The counsellor gives the client the task of continuing to do what has already proved to be helpful. The counsellor may also ask the client to think how he will remind himself to keep doing what he knows is helpful.

Some solution-focused counsellors routinely give tasks and question their clients about their homework. In the early years, probably due to the influence of Erickson among others, the giving of counsellor-designed tasks was more significant than it is today. The emphasis today is less upon the counsellor prescribing tasks and more on supporting clients in tasks which they themselves have designed.

When a client does not carry out an agreed task the counsellor is unlikely to give him another one, unless there is evidence this would be a good idea. Even where a client has not performed the task the counsellor can still pay him the compliment of knowing that it was not a good time to carry out the task. The counsellor may ask: 'What did you do instead?', 'When will you know it is a good time to perform the task?', 'What will be the sign for you?' The client may modify the task or do something else altogether. In this case the counsellor will be supportive. She may ask how the client decided what to do. 'How did you work that out?', 'Where did you get that idea from?' If it worked the counsellor will compliment the client on his initiative.

Where the counsellor has taken the leading role in designing the task she should ensure that the task is timely, appealing and realistic to the client. The client may have ideas about shaping it more to his circumstances.

THE FEEDBACK

Giving feedback about the session to the client is an important element in the solution-focused approach. When the client makes a contract the counsellor will explain that she will take a break approximately fifteen minutes before the session ends. During the break the counsellor will reflect on what has been said in the session. If she has someone else co-working with her she will consult with them. If the counsellor is working on her own she will take a break to reflect on the notes she has taken and to prepare the feedback. She may do this in the presence of the client or she may leave the room for five minutes. If a client shows signs of being anxious the counsellor may decide to omit the break and go directly into the feedback. Sometimes both the client and the counsellor feel mentally and emotionally tired towards the end of a session. The short break is welcomed on both sides as it gives them the chance to refocus before ending. Before taking the break the counsellor checks with the client to find out if there is anything else the client wants to say.

To the reader this delivering of the stone tablets may sound strange and out of keeping with the collaborative relationship described to this point. In certain hands the delivery of the feedback could look as if the counsellor is in the expert role. Much depends upon the spirit in which the counsellor gives the feedback. Since the core of the feedback consists of re-presenting to the client what he or she has already articulated there is less of the power dimension to it than it sounds. The counsellor uses her skills to summarize the session in a focused way. There is rarely anything new or fresh introduced.

The structure of the feedback consists of:

- compliments
- bridging statement
- summary of what is already happening that is helpful
- an agreed task or tasks.

Compliments

The feedback begins with the counsellor paying genuine, evidence-based compliments to the client. The counsellor will express appreciation for the qualities the client has shown in the way he has talked about his problems. These may include honesty, clarity, courage and straightforwardness. The counsellor will acknowledge that it took the client a lot of faith and courage to disclose painful material. Even where the client has been guarded and reticent in communicating they have shown courage in attending the session. There may have been pressures for the client not to trust a stranger with his problems. Giving compliments in an unpatronizing way often increases the sense of collaboration between the counsellor and the client. Genuine compliments as distinct from manipulative flattery help to motivate the client, especially clients who carry histories of failure and rejection. It would be interesting to research whether the counsellor paying compliments makes a difference to the client's perception of the therapeutic relationship. Does it affect the degree to which they cooperate with tasks they have been given? Does it affect final outcomes? In paying therapeutic compliments the counsellor has to be sensitive to the gender and cultural background of the client. For some clients direct personal compliments might make them feel uncomfortable. If offered too early compliments might feel like clumsy attempts to avoid hearing about the client's pain or failure. Overdoing compliments lessens the impact of them. In some cases this could foster a dependency in which the client needed his fix of positive strokes.

The counsellor will probably have paid the client small compliments (positive reinforcement) during the session, for example, when the counsellor responds to the client's news of exceptions to the problem or progress on the scale. When clients terminate counselling prematurely some of the positive feedback they have received will hopefully be remembered by them. At the very least it may empower them to return for counselling at a later date.

Bridging statement

After paying the client compliments the counsellor will summarize the client's goals: 'In the session you said that you wanted to improve your communication with your partner. Instead of withdrawing from her you said you wanted to include her more in your life and you wanted to try a few things out to make it better.'

Summary of what is already happening that is helpful

The counsellor summarizes any constructive action which the client has already reported as doing or planning to do. The counsellor will encourage the client to consolidate what is working.

Task giving

The counsellor may give the client one of the different types of task described earlier in this chapter. The following example of feedback incorporates the four elements:

Counsellor: I would like to say how helpful it has been to hear how you see the situation ... You have obviously thought about it very carefully and have made connections between what is happening at work and what has also happened at home (*compliment*).

It feels as if you are beginning to identify recurring patterns in your life which you would like to change and that you feel ready to try and change some of them now before things deteriorate (*bridging statement*).

One of the things which has come across clearly to me is that you recognize much earlier than you used to that you are starting to become stressed. Noticing when things are getting on top of you before they get out of control is a useful starting point. You mentioned how important it was for you to take exercise, to play music, to talk to your partner, to ask yourself whether this issue was going to be important in a week, a month or a year ... and that sometimes these activities helped you to get things into proportion. You also feel you are getting better at speaking up and taking a stand when you feel you are being taken advantage of at work, although that is still very difficult for you to do. Maybe the more you do it the easier it will get (*summary of what is helpful*).

From what you have said it seems to me that you have got lots of ideas already on how you can stop the buildup of stress. You could decide whether to use some or all of them this week. You need to be alert so that you know what to do before your stress gets out of control (*task*).

SECOND SESSIONS AND BEYOND

Each client's circumstances are unique; for some change is sudden and dramatic, for others it is slow and painful. Second sessions can be very different from the first. The classic solution-focused opening to a second session is for the counsellor to ask the client, 'What's better or what's different?' This question immediately focuses upon the theme of change. It registers the counsellor's expectation that at least some aspect of the problem has changed since the last session. Not all clients can immediately join a change-focused conversation, particularly those who need to off-load negative experiences and feelings. It is important that the counsellor gives sufficient time and space to them. Other clients, however, report changes and improvements. 'The purpose of each successive session is to assess change and to help to maintain it so that a solution can be achieved' (Lipchik and de Shazer, 1986: 96). The focus on change should not, however, be relentless and oppressive. Clients need to feel safe, respected and validated. They need to know that it is acceptable to return with stories of failure and despondency. It would be unhelpful for the counsellor to give the impression that she was only interested in success stories. This might put pressure upon clients to exaggerate improvements to please the counsellor. Some clients have misgivings about reporting change as they fear it will not last, others are hesitant because they fear that progress will result in the counselling ending.

The counsellor accepts the client unconditionally, irrespective of his rate of progress. She shows faith in the client who makes painfully slow progress. Counsellors cannot avoid having feelings about their clients' progress or lack of it and neither can the clients themselves. If the client succeeds in doing the task assigned the counsellor is likely to offer positive reinforcement even if only in his body language. For the client failure to make progress or to do their 'homework' may generate negative feelings reminiscent of old scripts. Some clients probably fail to return for further counselling sessions because they are embarrassed at not having completed their 'homework'. Janis (1983) sums up the dilemma of how the counsellor should respond to a client's progress or lack of it.

> Unless a counsellor elicits some degree of commitment to carry out a course of action, the clients are likely to remain relatively unaffected and will derive little benefit from the relationship as far as the common goals of counselling are concerned. If the practitioner makes no such demands, either explicitly or implicitly, the relationship of the client to the accepting counsellor will continue in a warm, friendly way but will be ineffectual. (p. 33)

A counsellor cannot avoid influencing his/her clients in one way or the other even when they are trying to remain neutral or impartial. In order to avoid undue influence the counsellor should try to be detached from the client's answers. The counsellor should not allow herself to have strong preferences for one answer over another. The counsellor should not try to convince a 'failing' client that the situation is not as bad as he says, nor should the counsellor try to persuade the client that he has achieved more than he thinks he has. The counsellor needs to be careful that she does not patronize clients.

Clients often do make significant changes in their behaviour or attitude following the first session. This may be due partly to the relief of sharing a concern with a non-judgemental listener. Going public may in itself alter the client's perception of the situation. Bringing the problem into a social context alters the client's relationship to it. The counsellor should not underestimate the impact of a relationship, however brief, which communicates care and understanding to the client. Talmon's (1990) research into single-session therapy demonstrated the significant impact even one session of counselling had on many clients.

In second and subsequent sessions, the counsellor aims to elicit how the client managed to make changes and to explore with them how they could maintain or expand these changes. When the client reports positive change(s) the counsellor asks the client to describe how he managed to make the change(s). In asking for details the counsellor implies that the client did something to bring about change. It was not the result of luck or accident.

EXAMPLE

Client:	It has been quite a good week. On Monday I had to go to a meeting and I managed to speak at it.
Counsellor:	That was one of the things you wanted. How did you do it?
Client:	It helped having my colleague there. She knew I was nervous and we had a good talk before the meeting.
Counsellor:	Was that your idea and was it helpful?
Client:	We were having a coffee the day before and she asked me about the meeting and we found out that we both hated going to it. I think that made me feel better, that it was not only me who had difficulties with the way it is run.
Counsellor:	So having that chat helped you on the day. What happened?
Client:	I had read this article about how to be effective in meetings. One of the things it said was that it helped if you found it hard to talk in meetings to prepare a question beforehand. Write it down if it helps and try to ask it in the first fifteen minutes before you get too anxious. So that is what I did.
Counsellor:	You managed to do it even though you still felt nervous.
Client:	It felt like breaking a barrier. I spoke three times. It was amazing. It was as if I had suddenly become visible instead of invisible.

Clients are more likely to own discoveries they have made for themselves. 'Real health is the discovery of an enhanced reality and new consciousness that comes from within and not from an external source' (Adams, 1998: 23). The counsellor helps the client to be aware of what they have learned by making changes. The counsellor seeks to consolidate the changes by helping the client to be as clear as possible about what worked and how they made it work. Then the counsellor will ask the client how they could maintain or even develop these changes. These questions relate to maintenance, learning and evaluation strategies.

Box 5.1 *Strategy questions*

Maintenance strategies
What needs to happen to keep you where you are?
What might stop you doing that?
How could you overcome that?
What would be worth repeating?
What do you think you need to keep on track?
What will be the first thing you do if you think the problem is coming back?
Who could help you at that time?
Learning strategies
Why did you decide to do that?
What has your experience in tackling the problem taught you about yourself?
What do you know is not helpful for you even if it might be helpful for other people?
If you know it does not work how will you stop yourself doing it again?
What could you do instead?
How will you remind yourself what to do next time?
Are you thinking of trying anything different as an experiment?
What have you learned about accepting some things and changing others?
How will you handle those parts over which you have no control?
How might you be able to distinguish between what you can change and what you cannot?
Evaluation strategies
How does counselling help you?
What difference do you think it has made?
Is this what you want to see happening in your life?
Looking back to our starting point are these still your goals or have they changed?
What do you think we should concentrate on more and what could we put on one side?
What do you think about the number of sessions we might need?
When do you hope to be able to stop coming?

In second and subsequent sessions the counsellor focuses on solutions by:

- revisting the miracle question
- scaling
- predictions

Revisiting the miracle question

Miracles change. Clients may become conscious that small pieces of the miracle are already beginning to happen or they may decide that they no longer want some part of the miracle.

Scaling

Clients may return for subsequent sessions to report their stress level (a) has improved, (b) is worse, (c) is still the same or (d) is better in some respects but the same or worse in others. Sometimes clients report there has been no progress but then cite evidence for what seems to the counsellor to be progress. Clients may see no connection between their reduced stress and the counselling which they have received. They may be sceptical about whether the improvement will last or they may attribute the improvement to an indefinable factor beyond their control.

If the client reports in subsequent sessions that things are worse or remained the same a typical dialogue may be:

Client:	I have had a bad time.
Counsellor:	Where do you feel you are on the scale this week?
Client:	I am about a 1.
	(*The client was 4 last time. Counsellors do not remind clients they were previously higher on the scale. They will remind them if they had been lower.*)
Counsellor:	So you've been having a hard time. How have you managed to keep at one when things were going against you?
Client:	I went through the motions. I went on to automatic pilot. I thought just let them get on with it.
Counsellor:	How did that make a difference for you?
Client:	They could see there was something wrong so they steered clear of me. That suited me fine.
Counsellor:	How was that helpful for you?
Client:	I had got to a screaming pitch. I felt it would not take much for me to break down. Just putting on a mask meant I could escape into thinking about better things.
Counsellor:	What sort of things?
Client:	I thought about how much I would like to get away for a few days. I would like to go anywhere for a break.
Counsellor:	Is there any chance that could happen?
Client:	It would take a lot of arranging.
Counsellor:	What would be the first thing that would need to happen?
	(*Further into the discussion*)
Counsellor:	Coming back to the scale, what else kept you at a 1 this week and stopped you feeling even worse?
Client:	I went to bed early.
Counsellor:	How did that help?
Client:	It was just an escape. I felt if I could sleep I could recharge my batteries.

The counsellor may ask what the client did which stopped him becoming a 0. She would then explore what the client is thinking of doing to keep at a 1 or to move up the scale.

If a client remains on a low point on the scale for some time the counsellor will ask him whether there is any advantage in this. 'Does it feel all right being there?', 'What do other people who are close to you think about it?' The client may feel it is acceptable to be on a low point given the circumstances. For example, it is a difficult time near to an anniversary of a bereavement.

EXAMPLE

Counsellor: I know it has been a bad week but how did you stop it being even worse?

Client: I wasn't coping with the children so I asked their father to come over and look after them for a while. I wanted to go to the cemetery on my own.

Counsellor: How did that help?

Client: It was very peaceful up there. I like to look after the grave and have a talk with my Mum and Dad.

Counsellor: About how things are going or just anything?

Client: I tell them all the news and ask my Mum what she thinks I should do. Sometimes I think she speaks to me in some way because when I come back I often know what to do.

Counsellor: It feels as if she understands and still wants to help you.

Client: It feels like it.

When clients are unclear what they are doing to make their situation better, it can be helpful to ask what they would do if they intended to make it worse. This can be followed up with the questions:

- What do you do to ensure you do not do that?
- From what you know about how the problem started, what have you learned which you would pass on to someone else?

Predictions

Clients who report that the change is random and beyond their control are asked to predict each evening whether tomorrow is going to be a good or a bad day for them (Kral and Kowalski, 1989). At the end of each day the client checks his prediction for its accuracy. If it was accurate the client tries to identify what shaped the day. If the prediction was inaccurate (the day was better than predicted) the client reflects upon the positive experiences which made it a better day than expected. If the day was worse than predicted the client identifies the avoidable trouble spots.

Clients might report progress but not in relation to the original problem. They may see no connection between their improved functioning and their presenting problem. As they focus on solutions there may be fewer and fewer references to the problem. Centring the attention on solutions seems to have the effect of extinguishing problem talk. The counsellor reinforces this direction. This influence has to be acceptable to the client otherwise the relationship will break down.

The counsellor builds on what the client is already doing. She helps the client to take the next small step towards his goal. That step may be towards making further progress or to maintain the progress already made. At the very least it will be to halt further deterioration. When the client relapses the counsellor reframes the relapse as an opportunity for regrouping resources and renewing strategies. The experience of a relapse can remotivate as well as demotivate the client. It can clarify how much the client wants, or is able, to move forward in a progressive way. The counsellor may ask the client:

- Do you need to do something different?
- Are your goals realistic?
- Is the timetable realistic?
- What did you do to stop it getting worse?
- How did you cope despite the problem not improving?

The counsellor evaluates with the client whether the counselling is making a difference. Berg (1991) suggests that counsellors need to:

1. Pay close attention to how new information from the client confirms the direction of the work or whether it offers new ideas about what to do or what not to do.
2. Think of this new information as adding to the larger picture and not necessarily as something the clients were trying to hide.
3. Be flexible and willing to change in the light of new information.

The counsellor's internal supervisor – their own focus of evaluation - engages in a process of monitoring the work. Box 5.2 suggests some questions which may also be used with the counsellor's external supervisor.

Box 5.2 *Questions for an internal supervisor*

Do the changes take the client in the direction she wants to go?
Are they important but unrelated to the client's goals?
Do they indicate that the goals need to be renegotiated?
What information is now available which was not previously available?
What difference does this information make?
Does the problem need to be redefined?
Do the client's current resources need to be reassessed?
Does this mean that the pace of the work should be accelerated or slowed down?

ENDINGS

Since most solution-focused work is brief (less than ten sessions) endings are frequent and different from those in long-term work. Endings are built in from the beginning. The issue of dependency rarely arises. The focus is always on the task – on the real world in which the client is trying to make changes. There is little attention to the internal world of the client or to any intra-session events. This outward-looking perspective means that clients tend not to see counselling as something which has value in itself but rather as a means to an end.

CHAPTER 6

Integrative Solution-Focused Stress Counselling

The solution-focused approach is used in a wide range of settings, for example: education (Durrant, 1993), mental health (Wilgosh, 1993), social work (George *et al.*, 1990), the probation service (Lee *et al.*, 1999) as well as in counselling and psychotherapy (O'Connell, 1998). It has been used with individuals, families (Berg, 1991), couples (Hudson and O'Hanlon, 1991) and groups (Aambo, 1997). It has been used successfully with problems such as drug and alcohol misuse (Berg and Miller, 1992), parent–child conflict (Metcalf, 1997) and sexual abuse (Dolan, 1991). It has been adapted for business, personal and spiritual development.

There is a substantial body of evidence to prove that counselling/psychotherapy is effective (Sloane *et al.*, 1975). There is also evidence that no one type of therapy model can claim superiority over the others (Smith *et al.*, 1980, Garfield and Bergin, 1994). As a result, a growing body of counsellors reject a single-model approach and choose to integrate interventions from different schools. Many argue each model has its own specific contribution to make to the richness and diversity of the field. For example, the psychodynamic model has taught counsellors about the hidden motives behind human behaviour and the crucial importance of early childhood. The cognitive behavioural model has highlighted the centrality of clients' goals and the type of thinking required to achieve them. The person-centred model has given counsellors a paradigm for the alliance between counsellor and client. The solution-focused model has given counsellors a deeper appreciation of the client's resources and a different way of relating the client's history to their future.

Different models appeal to different counsellors and clients. As counsellors, our knowledge of therapeutic processes demands we recognize this diversity. With few exceptions, existing research evidence does not allow us to identify 'what treatment, by whom, is most effective for this individual, with that specific problem, and under which set of circumstances' (Paul, 1967: 109). Some practitioners may believe in the superiority of their model and hold that others are defective but there is no evidence to justify such a position. The need to believe in the superiority of one's model may come from counsellors who need to reduce their sense of powerlessness and anxiety in the face of human distress. It does not come from the clients who improve regardless of the model. There are advantages in belonging to a single school of therapy. It brings membership of an elite. It confers a professional and social identity. This, in turn, may bring privilege, status and power. Some schools of therapy see themselves as higher up the hierarchical ladder than others. Membership of these schools brings exclusivity. Other practitioners take a more inclusive and liberal attitude. The British Association for Counselling and Psychotherapy (BACP), for example, advocates a broad approach. It accredits counsellors provided they work within their competence, are truthful in their claims about what they are doing and conduct themselves according to the BAC Code of Ethics and Practice.

The value of an eclectic approach to counselling and psychotherapy has been described by various authors – Dryden (1992), Garfield (1995) and Palmer and Woolfe (2000). Feltham (1997) describes the different attitudes counsellors take towards theoretical purity or integration between therapies. He summarises the eclectic position:

> I see that people have a wide variety of problems and that society itself is hardly a sanity-generating milieu; I see that hundreds of explanations are held up and as many solutions proposed, none of which seems wholly satisfactory or unequivocally effective: I believe that there is some sense and some nonsense in most therapies and I strive hard to see how each individual can best be helped by the more sensible bits from each. I do not believe the pursuit of theoretical or technical purity and separatism is healthy or credible. (p. 123)

Up to a point different models achieve similar ends, although they may use different routes to get there and different descriptions of how they did it. The description of how clients were helped may take various forms:

- interpretation of unconscious material
- uncovering of hidden family scripts and myths
- exploring transactional positions of parent, adult, child
- challenging of irrational beliefs or distorted thinking
- empathic reflections
- experiential reflection on exceptions to the problem.

In books, journals, videos and live presentations, solution-focused practitioners present their work with clients. Inevitably it is their successes which are portrayed. This can give the impression that doing therapy is simple and easy, that success is virtually guaranteed. This simplistic message may be delivered for commercial reasons but it is galling for counsellors wrestling with challenging and intractable cases who see few visible results for their efforts. It can also be depressing for practitioners who return from such presentations and try to imitate the experts, only to find that it does not work for them. A greater degree of professional humility is needed. Counsellors need to acknowledge and learn from our failures as well as our successes. No one form of therapy works for everyone. We need a balanced view of the efficacy of any model.

In the first section of this chapter I would like to explore those occasions when, in my experience, the solution-focused approach does not work. I also examine some of the assumptions made by the solution-focused approach.

When the model does not work in a specific case it could be argued it is due to the counsellor's lack of skill. Attaching responsibility to either the counsellor or the client is, however, inconsistent with the social constructionist philosophy behind the approach. According to social constructionism the therapeutic alliance is co-negotiated between the counsellor and the client. The quality of the interaction is the result of the use clients and counsellors make of language. As Van Deurzen-Smith (1988.) suggests:

> Every approach to counselling is founded on a set of ideas and beliefs about life, about the world, and about people. ... Clients can only benefit from an approach insofar as they feel able to go along with its basic assumptions (p.1).

Not all clients are able to meet the demands of the solution-focused approach. When clients cannot do so a negative outcome is predicted. In my experience the model works least well:

- When clients are unable to engage in solution talk. The timing may not be right. They may be too depressed to form a positive relationship or lack the imagination and energy to visualize the future. They may be unable to recall the positive memories necessary to answer solution-oriented questions. A client may feel the counsellor does not sufficiently understand how difficult their situation is or does not realize the force of the obstacles in the way of change. Some clients cannot or do not want to progress beyond problem talk. They want to be heard. They find problem talk helpful and they reject solution-oriented interventions. Solution-focused counsellors do appreciate the value of listening but they also want to ask clients questions about their resources and coping strategies. In some cases there is a mismatch between the needs of the clients and the processes of the model.
- When clients do not believe they exercise power and control in their lives. With such clients the counsellor may first use a cognitive approach to challenge their beliefs. The solution-focused approach assumes clients have at least a measure of power and control in their lives and if this is not acknowledged by them then the counselling will not be successful.
- When clients do not feel able to respond to conversation about their strengths and qualities. This may be a question of timing as the client may not feel heard enough but sometimes clients will be unable to accept positive feedback about themselves.
- When clients are vague about their goals. Solution-focused techniques can often help clients to clarify their concerns and their preferred outcomes. Although the counsellor does not need to have full knowledge of the client's problems it is difficult for the client to sustain motivation unless they can agree signs of progress.
- When clients have a vested interest and a hidden agenda in maintaining the *status quo*, for example, when a compensation case or a benefits tribunal hearing is pending and they need to prove they are still experiencing problems to win their case. Some clients need to prove how dire their situation is to obtain the

kind of help they need, e.g. admission to hospital.
- When clients are convinced they need to know why they have their problem before they can do anything about it. Although the solution-focused approach suggests that understanding may follow action, clients can have fixed ideas about how understanding should emerge, for example, by a detailed biographical exploration.
- When clients believe counselling has to be long and painful to be effective. Such clients do not believe that a form of therapy which is optimistic and even, at times, enjoyable could possibly be addressing the real issues.
- When clients seek guidance and advice in the firm belief the counsellor knows best.
- When clients want improvements but do not want to make any effort themselves.
- When clients do not allow the counsellor to engage with their material.
- When clients are preoccupied with the relationship with the counsellor.
- When clients are over-compliant and falsely report progress to gain the counsellor's approval.

Selekman (1997), in his work with families, presents three situations where he feels the need to expand the solution-focused model:

1. When parents change their ideas and behaviour towards the identified child client but the child's difficulties do not improve.
2. When the parents' treatment goals are achieved but they do not consider the changes in their child as significant. Their core beliefs about the child and the situation remain intact.
3. When there are several professionals involved with the case who are pessimistic about the parents' and the child's ability to change. (p. 13)

In Selekman's view these situations can be managed if the counsellor adopts a flexible approach. In the first situation, play and art therapy with the family and visualization and cognitive work with the child may be of benefit. The second situation he sees as resulting from counsellors pursuing too positive an approach, one which leaves clients feeling as if they have not been taken seriously. In the third situation it is important to attend to the concerns of pessimistic helpers and to recognize that there are always many different ways of viewing a case. He argues that a more tolerant and integrative approach 'increases our repertoire of interpretation schemes and offers us a broader range of therapeutic options' (p. 14).

The limitations of some key solution-focused principles also incline me towards a more integrative position.

1. Small change can lead to bigger change

Changing one element in a system does not guarantee the consequences will be helpful or constructive, at least in the short term. Changing behaviour or attitudes can bring negative effects as well. These may include further oppression, an increased sense of inadequacy or a heightened sense of how much progress remains to be made. Initiating change can trigger memories of past hurts, regrets, failures or losses.

2. Clients have the resources to deal with their problems

Clients vary enormously in terms of their resourcefulness. Some have access to a wide range of personal and social resources, others lack social networks or prior experience of successfully using resources. In a crisis or under severe stress clients are often unable to mobilize their normal resources. Hobfoll (1998) defined stress as being a threat to the resources required for personal or group survival. He predicted stress would occur when an individual failed to receive a return on resources which had been invested, for example, when a person is made redundant after years of committed service to an employer with a subsequent loss of income and status. In some cases clients simply do not possess the information or skills to cope with the challenge the situation poses. They may cope for a time while they are hopeful and optimistic about finding a new job but once that possibility recedes they cannot adjust to the new threat their situation presents. Having invested so much of themselves in their work they find it difficult to find meaning in a society which largely defines people by their occupation.

Stressed clients may need help to learn and acquire new skills for coping. They may need to be taught how to relax or to be given techniques for stopping negative thoughts. They may need ideas on how to manage their time. They may need basic information about the physiological effects of stress or an understanding of the 'fight or flight' mechanism. They are likely to need specialist and accurate knowledge about the job market and their prospects within it.

3. Therapy should be as brief and as simple as possible

Not all clients are suitable for brief counselling. It is unethical to offer clients a 'one size fits all' approach. It should be a treatment of choice and not imposed for economic reasons on all clients. Some clients require and benefit from long-term therapy. Some respond better to a psycho-educational or supportive, person-centred approach. For some clients change is slow and uneven. Clients need to give informed consent to the counselling they are offered and they need the relevant information upon which to base their decision.

Solution-focused practitioners subscribe to the principle 'do something different if things are not working'. So when a client is unable to cooperate with a solution-focused approach the counsellor should find alternative ways to work with the client. This could be a referral for long-term therapy or a referral to another therapist who uses a different approach.

4. If it is not broken do not fix it

This principle discourages the counsellor from widening the client's agenda. However, there is a danger that the client will not be allowed to view their situation holistically. By this I mean the principle could lead to a fragmentation or compartmentalization of the client's life. The belief that something which is not broken does not require attention fails to take into account the need for maintenance.

It seems inconsistent with another solution-focused principle – if it works keep doing it. Part of the solution could be to maintain what is working and to keep improving it.

5. Counselling is change focused

Having a clear focus is important but there is also a danger of fostering a 'fast food' approach which colludes with a client's drive towards change. This drive for change could be part of the problem. Clients may be trying to fit social norms which are unreasonable or unhealthy. They may be trying to meet someone else's demands for them to change. For example, it may be more important in the long run for a client to accept herself for who she is, rather than who someone else thinks she ought to be. It can be a legitimate goal to resist further change. It can be wise to consolidate or to 'simply be'. There can be a relentlessness in the solution-focused approach. It can communicate to the client a message that if she is not an activist for change there is something wrong. This aspect of the model colludes with the contemporary spirit which sets results above process and the outer world above the inner.

6. Solutions fit the person not the problem

Does the approach ignore the social structures in which people live? Does it take an individualistic stance? Does the approach amount to a form of social control because it fails to address contextual issues? Does it only help clients to adapt to the *status quo*?

Clients' goals are accepted without reference to the social conditions which created them. For example, the counsellor addresses a female client's goal to overcome an eating disorder without addressing the social influences on women to conform to the dominant culture's idea of what women should look like. Clients are of course individuals and should not be treated as part of an homogeneous group but the meaning of their problem is only comprehensible in a social context. As Hobfoll (1998) states in regard to stress,

> When appraisals are made regarding threats to the self, they are contextualized within social standards and markers, and people look to their social environment for feedback about the threat, preferred responses, and solace. (p. 52)

None of the leading proponents of the model discuss the effect of gender, race, class and sexuality in their work. Some advocate that such issues are irrelevant unless the client specifically raises them. A form of social blindness is advocated. This flies in the face of what we have learned over the past twenty years of counselling and psychotherapy – namely that black clients, for example, drop out of therapy quicker than white clients (Abramowitz and Murray, 1983).

Goddard (1996) criticizes the solution-focused approach on the grounds that:

(a) By focusing on behavioural change rather than on feelings there is a danger that change will be superficial. As a result clients may develop a false sense of control and may only exchange one set of problems for another.

(b) It depends too much on what the client tells the counsellor and does not utilize the counsellor's intuition enough. Clients may seek the counsellor's approval

and comply with the process and the tasks given to them without engaging authentically.
(c) It colludes with clients' expectations that therapy could be brief which, in her eyes is 'more a reflection of the general lack of psychological insight and education and merely demonstrates the subtle introjection of a culture that places action above reflection and rates progress over process'. (p. 410)

THE SOLUTION-FOCUSED CONTRIBUTION

To my mind the specific contribution of the solution-focused model is that:

- it acts as a corrective to approaches which make negative assumptions and inferences about clients
- it gives counsellors choices about where to start with clients. For example, some clients do not need to begin with history
- it encourages counsellors to maintain a balance between problem exploration and solution construction
- it nurtures hope and optimism
- it enables clients to break out of a problem–dominated narrative
- it taps into the intuitive, creative and imaginative side of the brain
- it helps clients to be specific in the way they formulate problems and the changes they want
- it often gives clients immediate rewards and encouragement to continue in therapy
- it brings out the resourcefulness of clients
- it makes full use of their uniqueness
- the techniques can be used by counsellors who do not want to commit themselves to using the whole model
- its concern for the individual agendas of clients and its emphasis on minimal interference reduces the danger of dependency
- it highlights the role of the counsellor in shaping the narratives of clients
- it is an accessible form of therapy.

THE COMMON FACTORS APPROACH

Although it makes sense from a commercial point of view to promote the differences between therapies, research suggests it is the common factors across the therapies which are more significant. Cramer (1992: 153) identifies a number of processes common to all therapies:

1. Counselling gives clients an opportunity for experiential learning in which they become aware of the discrepancy between their assumptions about the world and reality. This new learning opens up the possibilities of change.
2. There is a release of hope created by the client's faith in the counsellor and which is reinforced by the counsellor.
3. The counselling process gives the client a series of success experiences which enhance their sense of competence.

4. Counselling gives clients a conceptual framework in which they realize their problems are not unique and others care and understand them.

According to Lambert and Bergin (1994):

- 40 per cent of the variance in psychotherapy outcome can be attributed to the operation of extra therapeutic factors, such as the client's environment and life chances.
- 30 per cent to the therapeutic relationship.
- 15 per cent to specific factors relating to models.
- 15 per cent to the effect of placebo factors.

The client is the most important variable. The above factors are found in the solution-focused approach in the following ways:

Extra therapeutic factors

The solution-focused approach gives priority to the ways in which the client makes and sustains changes. It identifies and validates what the client is already doing right. It works with the client's unique frame of reference and stays close to the client's agenda. It attends to the client's language and seeks to match it. It recognizes that life itself can be a healing agent for change.

The therapeutic relationship

The relationship is characterized by the counsellor's respect for and validation of the client's experiences. It is an open and cooperative relationship. It is person centred in its acceptance of the client's definition of the problem and in its adherence to the client's goals. Solution-focused therapists who initially placed great emphasis upon the techniques of the model are now recognizing the fundamental importance of the quality of the therapeutic relationship.

Placebo factors

Placebo is a medical term used to describe the benefit a patient gains from the belief that what he or she is taking will produce good results, even if the medication prescribed is, for example, only water. Clients may experience benefit from making an appointment to see a counsellor. The act of sharing concerns with the counsellor may immediately produce feelings that the situation could improve. Catching the hope conveyed by the counsellor is a placebo effect. Clients often feel better and make improvements in their situation after they have gone public with their problem.

In terms of expectations the solution-focused counsellor consciously creates a climate of change. He aims to generate hope and create positive expectations in the client. The model sets change at its heart. It encourages the client to notice change prior to the first session. It gives the client the task of looking out for change. Increasing expectancy of change usually leads the client to find evidence for it. This in turn encourages them to find further evidence. Interventions, such as exception seeking, imply change is within reach or has already happened. The model implies change comes about in many different ways but usually requires the client to act positively. It is forward looking and optimistic. It gives the client credit for success. These placebo factors need to be tempered to the needs of each client. Too forceful an emphasis on change will discourage and depress some clients. By paying attention to the client's verbal and non-verbal responses the counsellor knows when to back off. He knows when to tone down the positive emphasis. On occasions he may even take a more negative position than the client to encourage them to argue the case for the positive. The blending of the placebo ingredients should follow a different recipe for every client.

INTEGRATING DIFFERENT TECHNIQUES

Techniques are used within the context of a therapeutic relationship. The therapeutic relationship has the following characteristics:

- respectful and attentive listening
- reflective silences
- empathy
- warmth
- care
- gentleness
- humour
- genuineness
- immediacy
- acceptance.

In this section I would like to outline how techniques from other therapeutic traditions can be incorporated into a solution-focused model.

Solution-focused counselling and cognitive behavioural techniques

Cognitive behavioural interventions have been widely used in the field of stress management (Milner and Palmer, 1998). In my experience they can be integrated into a solution-focused approach. They can be used with clients whose negative and disempowering beliefs about themselves prevent them from engaging in meaningful solution talk or action. The following techniques can be used: Thought stopping, replacing negative imagery, challenging beliefs, adopting techniques from other therapies, information giving, and the use of a stress line.

THOUGHT STOPPING

Clients who are disabled by recurring unwanted negative thoughts need techniques to regain control of their thought processes. In learning how to block unwanted thoughts from their minds the client is encouraged to employ a range of images and actions which act as clear signals to engage in diversionary thinking:

- a red traffic signal
- a stop sign
- saying 'Stop' out loud.

For the client the first step is to become aware of the trancelike state into which they fall when dwelling upon negative thoughts, the second step is to generate the thought-stopping signal and the third step is to replace the negative thinking with more life-enhancing thoughts.

REPLACING NEGATIVE IMAGERY

Clients may be disturbed by intrusive negative imagery which causes them anxiety or depression. They need a stock of alternative images to employ at such times. These may be found in:

- memories which the client can replay in his or her head – memories of pleasant holidays, hobbies, events or people
- images of a time when the client felt strong/peaceful/relaxed
- replays of the client's favourite television programme or film
- images of places which have a calming or relaxing effect – the sea, the countryside.

When countering stressful thoughts the client can immerse herself in positive images. She may imagine the positive scene through all the senses – smelling the smells, seeing the sights and hearing the sounds. When faced with a particularly stressful situation the client can learn to prepare for it by calling up images which help to put them in an appropriate mood.

CHALLENGING BELIEFS

Many clients' problems are caused by the way they view them. It is their interpretation of events which leads them to feel anxious or depressed. How they interpret events is a product of their history. From a social constructionist point of view there is no 'right' way of interpreting reality. There are always different explanations one could choose.

Clients may choose explanations which trap them in their problems. They may do this by:

- personalizing situations
- always looking for negatives and ignoring the positives
- exaggerating
- selectively processing information – ignoring information which does not fit
- jumping to conclusions
- mind reading
- engaging in extreme – all or nothing thinking
- generalizing from the particular.

These and many other mental habits result in clients 'creating' their own reality in ways which cause them to feel badly and lead them to act problematically.

EXAMPLE

Kate greets her manager in the corridor. He ignores her and walks past. She could decide that (a) her manager was discourteous and unfriendly, (b) had a hearing problem or (c) was preoccupied. As a consequence of which option she chooses she may feel angry, sympathetic or unconcerned. She may blame herself for the incident – I should have spoken more clearly. As a result of the encounter she may conclude that she is not liked by her manager and must do more to impress him or conversely she may feel demotivated. She may decide not to greet him next time she meets him. How she feels and how she acts depends upon how she reads the situation.

The solution-focused counsellor will help the client to interpret events in ways which allow constructive change to follow. Explanations which make the situation more solvable will be preferred over ones which make change less likely in the short and in the long term.

O'Hanlon and Beadle (1994: 29) identifies four types of explanations which the solution-focused counsellor discourages the client from adopting:

1. Explanations which blame clients for their problems.
2. Explanations which invalidate clients' experiences.
3. Explanations which preclude the possibilities for change.
4. Explanations which remove or block the recognition of personal accountability.

The solution-focused counsellor challenges clients' distorted beliefs in a less direct way than the confrontational psycho-educational style of the cognitive therapist by:

- Focusing on exceptions to the problem. This challenges the client's beliefs about its all-pervasive nature.
- Giving the client credit for success. This implies the client also has to assume an appropriate level of responsibility for the problem.
- Expressing curiosity about the process by which a client reached a dogmatic and rigid belief.
- Inserting doubt into a client's fixed beliefs. The counsellor suggests there are alternative explanations or casts doubt on whether a totally convincing explanation could be found or would prove helpful.
- Reframing. The counsellor reframes a client's perception by placing it in a different context and in so doing changes its meaning. For example, the client may see himself as weak and pathetic because he does not fight back when his boss is verbally abusive towards him. This could be reframed to the client as 'self-control exercised under extreme provocation while you wait to find a strategy which will work'. The counsellor will explore the ways in which the client could translate this strong, clever, self-controlled self-belief into a strategy which would counter the behaviour of the boss.

- Externalizing the problem. The client is encouraged to talk as if the problem is 'out there' and to discuss it in terms of how it attacks and tries to control the person. This gives the client a new way of seeing the problem. Seeing it from a different position opens the possibility of having a different type of relationship with it. Clients can learn to recognize when stress or anxiety is about to attack. They can explore how strong an influence stress is perceived to have over their lives and which strategies are most successful at repelling the stress attack. Viewing stress from this vantage point helps the client to see the stress in an interactional context and steers him or her away from explanations which look towards the 'inner' life.

ADAPTING TECHNIQUES FROM OTHER THERAPIES

1. *Empty chair*. The Gestalt technique of inviting the client to engage in a dialogue with an absent person can be used in a solution-focused way.

In the example below the client uses the empty chair to 'communicate' with a colleague who does not value her work contribution.

Counsellor: What would you like to say to your colleague if he was sitting there on that chair?

Client: I would want to tell him he is wrong about me.

Counsellor: Would you like to say that to him?

Client (*to empty chair*):

You have never tried to see things from my point of view. You made up your mind without giving me a chance. You don't see all the things I do for you. You only look for things to criticize.

Counsellor: Would you like to tell him what it is he does not know about you?

Client: You do not know how much I cover up for your mistakes. You have no idea how much I have to smooth things over with people you have upset. You do not know how much stress you cause me and everyone else in the office.

Counsellor: What difference would it make to you if you said something like that to him?

Client: I'd probably get sacked!

Counsellor: How would you act if you *imagined* you had said that to him?

Client: I would probably stop covering up for him so much. I would not suffer in silence so much.

Counsellor: Are you thinking of covering up less for him?

Client: I am thinking about it.

The empty chair technique can also be used to facilitate a dialogue between two conflicting sides of the client's personality.

Client: At times I feel I have done really well with my life, at others I feel full of regrets for opportunities I have missed.

Counsellor (*using the empty chair*):

What would you like to say to that side of you which feels regrets?

Client: You did what you thought was right at the time. It's easy to be wise after the event.

Counsellor: What difference would it make to you if you took that message on board more?

Client: I would be easier on myself and give myself more credit for surviving.

Counsellor: What else would you like to say to the regretful part?

Client: Nothing in life is lost. Even when things don't work out you can always use what happens to you at some other point in your life. I really believe that.

Counsellor: Is that something you need to remind yourself about when the negative side takes over? How could you do that?

2. *Projective techniques.* Several models of therapy encourage clients to use objects such as stones, pictures, buttons and other everyday items to access feelings. A solution-focused approach will give priority to clients accessing feelings and thoughts likely to change the problem-dominated story clients hold about themselves.

3. *Writing exercises.* Many different types of therapy encourage clients to keep journals or diaries which record the progress of their problem. A solution-focused journal will record not only descriptions of how the problem happened but also examples of exceptions, strategies and client strengths. Yvonne Dolan (1998) has produced many solution-focused writing exercises for clients, adapted versions of which are reproduced here with permission.

(a) Write, read and burn

- Write a description of an intrusive image or thought which you find stressful on a piece of paper.
- Read it aloud to a supportive person or, if no one is available, to yourself while imagining the support of that person.
- Tear up and burn the piece of paper.

(b) Letter from the future

Choose a time in the future and imagine you are writing to a good friend. Date the letter. In the letter describe how much you are enjoying your life now that you are not so stressed. Describe where you are living, your relationships, how you spend your time, how you are feeling and thinking. Describe how you have overcome or come to terms with the problems currently affecting you.

The letter is not to be sent, it is for the client. Although there may be a wish list element to the letter, clients can often use it to decide how they could be living a less stressful life.

(c) A rainy day letter

This letter is written at a time when the person is not stressed. It is for use when the person is not coping with life. In the letter write down:

- activities you find comforting, relaxing or enjoyable

- your qualities and strengths
- your priorities and the beliefs to which you hold
- your hopes and dreams for the future
- the names of people who are important to you and who are part of your solution
- what you need to remember at times of stress – these may include thoughts and actions.

(d) Rewriting negative messages

Consider what negative or destructive message from your past interferes with your confidence or your positive feelings about your life. Now think of a new and healthy message you would like to receive instead. Write down the new message several times with each hand until it begins to feel like a familiar part of your belief system. Now share this message with someone else.

INFORMATION GIVING

Some counsellors give or recommend to clients books and leaflets relevant to their problems. With clients suffering from stress the counsellor imparts the basic facts about stress to raise the client's self-awareness. This can be therapeutic and empowering in itself. The information will include:

- the signs and symptoms of stress
- the ways distress can lead to ill-health
- the physiological changes which accompany emotions and behaviour
- the pharmacological basis of treatment for stress-related disorders
- the rationale for coping strategies, such as relaxation training
- the role of social networks
- anxiety and anger management techniques
- the need for specific changes in living patterns.

Many clients can access the Internet for information and support on all aspects of stress. They may use forums and chat rooms to discuss their situation with others and to ask experts for their opinions.

STRESS LINE

The counsellor invites the client to draw a lifeline of stressful experiences he or she can recall. When it is completed the counsellor asks the client questions about the coping strategies used at those times and how they feel these episodes have influenced their approach to the current stress experience.

In discussion with the counsellor Martin (32) chose a number of significant stress episodes.

1. His father leaving the family home when he was 12 was a major blow to his confidence and self-esteem. He regretted the absence of a role model during his adolescence. Looking back now he thinks it has made him an independent person who knows he has to look after himself. This can be a positive strength at times but

Figure 6.1 *Martin's stress line*

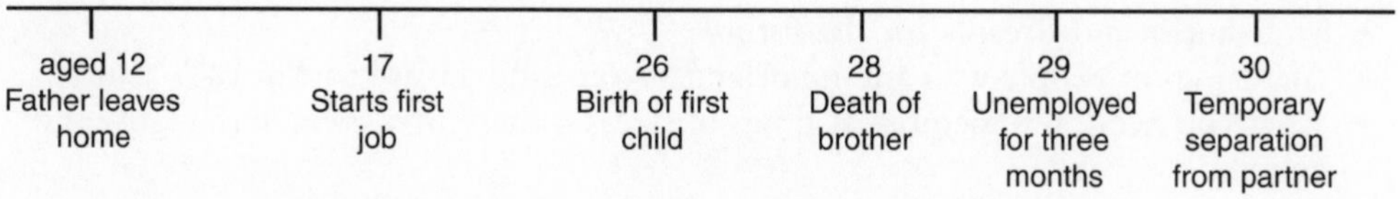

aged 12	17	26	28	29	30
Father leaves home	Starts first job	Birth of first child	Death of brother	Unemployed for three months	Temporary separation from partner

it can also make him appear self-contained and unwilling to accept help from his partner.

2. The second episode Martin chose to highlight was the anxiety he felt when he started his first job. He was desperate to be accepted by his work colleagues. Joining the heavy drinking culture of the workplace seemed to him essential. When he began to realize that his drinking was getting out of control, he managed to cut back his drinking over a period of time without losing his place in the group.

3. The third episode Martin chose was the time in his relationship with his long-term partner after the birth of their first child. A combination of sleepless nights, adapting to parental roles, coping with the baby when she was sick, worries about money and reduced quality adult time caused high levels of stress and mutual dissatisfaction with the relationship. Although they split up for a short while they came back together and decided they would pull through this bad patch together. They both felt they had seen a side of each other's character they had not seen before. Martin was pleased he had not run away from problems as he had on previous occasions but had found depths of commitment, perseverance and self-sacrifice previously missing from his life.

From discussing these and other stress events Martin was able to identify coping strategies he had used before, strengths he could utilize and beliefs which were important to him.

These are only a few examples of how techniques used in problem-focused therapies can be adapted for use within a solution-focused framework.

CHAPTER 7
Counselling Relationships under Stress

In this chapter I explore how the solution-focused model can be used for counselling relationships under stress.

COUPLE COUNSELLING

When people are stressed there are inevitable consequences for their work and personal relationships. The threat which generates the stress may arise in either sector of a person's life. An imbalance between work and personal life is likely to create stress at some point. Many middle-aged people, particularly men, who have invested a lot of themselves in their work may find they have done so at the cost of their personal life. By the time they realize they have neglected to nurture their closest personal relationships it is often too late to recover them.

Conflict between couples arises because they lack a sufficiently relevant repertoire of skills to resolve and accommodate their differences. They have become stuck in fixed roles, often with routine patterns of predictable behaviour. Since people are in a constant state of change, roles which once fitted no longer fit. When one partner wants to change role, the other may be unable or unwilling to allow this to happen. It raises anxieties about dependence and independence, separation and intimacy. For a solution-focused approach to work the couple need to be willing to experiment. At least one partner needs to be willing to break the impasse. One partner has to be a customer for change.

Both partners are likely to need to change the way they interpret the dynamics of the relationship. They need to move from blame to accountability. They need to extend their interpersonal repertoire. Inevitably they need to establish new communication patterns.

Although in practice much relationship counselling takes place with only one partner present, there are distinct advantages for the counsellor in having both partners present.

- It enriches the one-dimensional picture only one partner can give.
- It generates alternative ways of understanding the relationship.
- It provides a direct opportunity to observe the couple's interactions as distinct from second-hand reports about them.
- It enables difficult and painful conversations between the partners to advance much further than when the couple are on their own. Previous conversations between them may have degenerated into verbal warfare or violence. The counsellor is able to act as mediator.

The solution-focused approach to couples counselling is characterized by:

1. *Brevity*. The solution-focused approach aims to help the couple in crisis to find ways to build a momentum for change. The counsellor does not seek labels for the couple's behaviour or conduct a lengthy investigation into the couple's history.
2. *Simplicity*. The counsellor does not try to formulate a theory to explain the couple's difficulties. Such theories can be complex guesswork and bring with them implications of blame for one or other partner. If the source of the problem is 'traced' to families of origin this is just as likely to have a disempowering as a liberating effect. Relationship analysis is nearly always disputed by one or other partner and can have a divisive effect. A solution-focused approach represents minimal intrusion into the couple's private lives.
3. *No-blame*. It can be a challenge to engage the cooperation of the partner who feels blamed by the other or to keep the peace between two angry parties who blame their unhappiness on one another. Accountability replaces blame.
4. *Positive dialogue*. While validating the couple's complaints and negativity, the counsellor declares an unequivocal positive stance in relation to the couple's future. The counsellor encourages the couple to build upon their strengths and to employ transferable skills from other areas of their lives.
5. *Subjectivity*. The social-constructionist view is that neither partner can be objective about their relationship. What they bring to the conversation is personal truth-subjective perception.
6. *Future orientation*. The couple may be unable to agree a definition of the problem. They may disagree over its severity, its duration, its meaning, its consequences or its very existence. This conflict can take a considerable time to resolve, if it can be resolved at all. In the solution-focused approach it is less important for the couple to reach a consensus about the problem and more important they reach a consensus about the desired future. No matter how the problem came about – whether its roots lie in the families of origin or in a personal deficit of one party or in social circumstances, they still have to find a way forward which meets the needs of the two parties.

In many respects the solution-focused method works well with couples. It is a useful tool for helping couples to free themselves from the recurring cycles in which they find themselves. The solution-focused questions written about elsewhere in this book can be very powerful when answered by a couple in one another's presence. Hearing the other person's answer to the miracle question can be a revelation. A joint search for exceptions can be something quite new and different. Using and sharing scales to measure progress can give a clearer understanding of what works and what does not work for each of them. Scaling can give the couple a clear focus for the work. Tasks can be designed by the couple in collaboration with the counsellor which build upon what they are doing right and the need to do something different.

Counsellors use the past to find keys for the future. They may ask the couple what brought them together in the first place and invite them to explore important times since then when their relationship was better than it is now. When the couple begin to talk about how they met and what attracted them to each other, there can be a shift in feelings and thinking.

- How/Where did you two meet?
- What attracted you to each other?
- How did you have good times together?
- I know a lot has happened since then but what would you like to recapture from that time in your lives?
- What does your partner still do that makes you appreciate/love him/her?
- What do you love about your partner? (The counsellor might need to give some warning of this question!)

Couples need joint/mutual goals as well as personal goals. They may have clear ideas what they want for themselves but be less clear what they want together. As well as having a personal answer to the miracle question they need a joint vision of a future together with their mutual needs being met more than they are at present.

Couples may be helped by linking the way they view each other with how they treat each other. A change in the way they interpret and label each other's behaviour opens possibilities for acting differently.

- How are you viewing your partner in ways which affect the way you treat her/him?
- When you begin to think negatively about your partner are you ever able to stop yourself acting negatively towards her/him?
- If you were to think of your partner differently how do you think it would alter the way you treat her/him?

Zimmerman *et al.* (1997: 125) describe a six-session model of solution-focused group work with couples.

Session One
The facilitators explain the key principles and techniques of the model. They negotiate ground rules. They initiate discussion of the myths which affect relationships. There is instruction on how to set effective goals.
Session Two
The participants are asked about any changes or differences in their relationship since the previous week. There is a focus on small changes which the couple may fail to notice. They are helped to sharpen their goals. The facilitators concentrate upon what works for the couples.

Session Three
There is continuing focus on the changes the couples have experienced since the previous session. Partners are encouraged to notice changes in the other person. The facilitators discuss how couples could identify problem patterns in their relationship and how they might develop strategies to interrupt them.
Session Four
This session deals with failure – when attempts to change problem patterns do not work.
Session Five
This session explores how changes in the couple's relationships are affecting other areas of their lives, for example: work, children, friends and extended family.
Session Six
The agenda for this session includes strategies for coping with setbacks, celebrating successes and generating hopes for the future. Time is also spent on ending the group.

Throughout the life of the group couples were encouraged to become more aware of the changes taking place in their relationships. Each couple had homework assignments to complete. The project involved twenty-three couples who participated in the groups and a comparison group of thirteen couples who were given the same pre- and post-test questionnaires to complete but who did not receive any help other than a discussion of their scores at the end of the six-week period. The research showed that the scores of the couples in the treatment group relating to overall affectional expression and satisfaction improved significantly during the life of the group. Partners reported the following changes:

- having shorter, less intense arguments
- more acceptance of each other's differences
- increased physical affection
- making more time for each other
- more effective problem solving including less blaming
- greater focus on solutions
- a greater sense of calm
- a capacity for spontaneity in the relationship
- an awareness of problematic patterns.

Lipchik and Kubicki (1996) have written about using a solution-focused approach with couples where there has been domestic violence.

FAMILIES UNDER STRESS

Families are subject to tremendous pressures in contemporary society. These pressures include:

- privatization of family life
- impact of work stress on marital and parental relationships

- changing roles of men and women
- pressure on children to perform academically
- increased expectations of personal relationships
- decreasing consensus on matters of belief and morality
- cross-cultural tensions between traditional families and western values
- fragmentation of community
- loosening of extended family ties
- poverty/unemployment
- depressed environment.

In this book there is scope only to touch upon the application of solution-focused work to families. There is extensive treatment of its use with families in Berg (1991 and 1994), Metcalf (1997), Selekman (1997), and Turnell and Edwards (1999). It has also been used by family support workers to promote positive parenting (Colledge, 1999). There is increasing recognition that parenting is a complex set of social skills. Adults with poor experience of parenting in their original families often lack the range of skills needed to care for and support a child's growth. Social deprivation creates and compounds this deficit. Poverty, a failed education, limited employment opportunities, impoverished environment and bad housing put intolerable strains on parents. Parents become suspicious and defensive towards middle-class professionals who do not understand the stresses they are under and whom they fear will take their children into care. Family support workers often have to work hard to earn their trust.

Television, popular psychology literature and the Internet offer a flood of advice to parents, much of it contradictory or unhelpful. Solutions for common child problems are delivered in a 'one size fits all' way. What the solution-focused approach advocates is collaboration with the parent in the search to find a solution which fits this child and this parent. Solution-focused family workers regard parents as partners. Even when workers are statutorily involved in child abuse investigations they aim to seek the cooperation of the parents (Turnell and Edwards, 1999).

A group of family support workers recently trained in the solution-focused approach reported on how it had changed their approach to parents.

'I help parents to find their own solutions, letting them find answers and not just me giving advice.'

'I can now work through ideas and solutions and empower the client – instilling confidence and rectifying a problem before it progresses further.'

'A parent was describing how her son had tantrums and how could she improve his behaviour as there had been complaints from neighbours as they could hear him banging his head on the floor. I asked if there were times when he didn't have tantrums and she said when he had space outside either at Parent and Toddler or when she visited her dad and he could play in the garden. She then offered the suggestion herself that it was helpful when she had a routine. She said that even though it took effort it helped to take her son out every day to prevent him from becoming frustrated in the flat and therefore being more prone to having tantrums. I complimented her for thinking out what would be best for all concerned.'

'A parent was concerned about her son's aggressive behaviour in the home although he behaved very well at playgroup. She described some failed strategies she had tried such as keeping him out in the porch, but he was so strong he had broken the glass. When I enquired further the mother was able to come up with instances when she had the situation under control. She was not able to pinpoint what had made the difference and she felt her son's behaviour did not always follow a pattern. She agreed to keep a record of times when she managed him better and to think about how she had done it. She also thought she would continue to do those things which were already working.'   (Colledge, 1999: 8)

In the solution-focused approach to families the parents and the children are invited to bring along anyone they think could be helpful in solving the problem. Everyone is invited to take an active part in the discussion. No one is allowed to remain in the detached observer role. Children are normally asked questions first to ensure their voices are not lost. Each family member is asked the same questions and invited to comment on each other's answers. The emphasis is on eliciting the expertise within the family. This expertise could be found in the children as well as the adults. Selekman (1997) identifies many studies of children which reveal their resourceful approach to problem solving.

   We all know how much our childhood affects us throughout our lives. We did not all have an equal or fair start. Some of us were wanted, loved and well cared for. Others were unwanted, neglected and even abused. Those who did not receive good parenting may feel they are also going to be poor parents. They may predict for themselves the same problems, illnesses, failures and personality defects of their parents. However, human beings are resilient and resourceful and most people do recover from bad starts. Although there are ways we are similar to our parents (e.g. we may look like one of them), we are also our own people and can make our own choices. To feel empowered, to take control of our lives, we need to have a sense of *our difference* from our families of origin, as well as an appreciation of what was good in what we inherited.

- In which ways are you similar to each of your parents or childhood caregivers?
- In which ways do you differ from them?
- Of those ways you are like her/him/them, which do you value most?
- Which ways do you value least?
- In those ways in which you are not like her/him/them which do you value most?
- Which ways do you value least?
- In terms of how this shows itself in your day-to-day life, what do you want to do more of and what less of?

Adapted from an exercise in *One Small Step* by Yvonne Dolan (1998: 126). Reproduced with permission.

SOLUTION-FOCUSED GROUPS

The literature describes how groups can be effectively run using solution-focused principles and techniques: with offenders (Lee *et al.*, 1999), with parents (Selekman, 1991), with couples (Zimmerman *et al.*, 1997) and with psychiatric patients (Gilbey and Turner, 1993).

Solution-focused stress groups may be run on a preventative or remedial basis. There is an overlap between the two as in any preventative group there will be participants who are already suffering from high levels of stress.

How does a solution-focused group differ from other therapy groups?

1. The main difference is the degree of attention the facilitator and group members pay to the strengths, strategies and successes of individual members. Each person is encouraged to participate actively in seeking out, owning and celebrating exceptions to the problem. The frequent use of therapeutic compliments creates an affirming and supportive climate.
2. The aim of the group is to communicate to its members the belief they have power to control their stress levels. Some people may have avoided self-help groups in the past because they saw them as talking shops for inadequate people to pour over their problems. They believed that the experience of listening to other people's problems would only serve to reinforce their own. In a solution-focused group members are encouraged to adopt positive attitudes and focus on successes not problems.
3. The group helps the individual to develop well-formed goals and to seek evidence of progress in small steps.
4. The group's search for solutions means that individuals can borrow solutions from others.
5. The ordinariness of solution-focused discussions makes them more accessible to participants who feel anxious about talking in a group. Questions focus on concrete matters rather than on abstract material. For example, 'How did you cope when you felt really worried?' People who are comfortable with imaginative and descriptive material (right-brain ability) are able to answer such questions, whereas they may struggle with verbal, rational, analytic material which demands left-brain skills (Washburn, 1994).
6. Their views and opinions are not analysed but validated. Participants come to realize there are no right or wrong answers, only different ways of seeing things.

STRESS MANAGEMENT GROUPS

Stress management groups typically offer a skills based programme which covers issues such as:

- basic information about the stress process
- cognitive techniques such as stress innoculation
- time management skills
- assertiveness skills
- delegation skills
- relaxation/exercise/diet.

(Reynolds and Briner, 1996)

These groups may be offered to all employees as part of staff development. There is therefore a considerable variation in the agendas which participants bring. For some it is an opportunity to express their feelings about the organization and the factors which they see as causing stress, for example, lack of resources, work overload or role conflict. For others, whose stress level has reached a critical point, it can be a cathartic public expression of their problems. Their sense of failure and inadequacy will be reinforced if the group facilitator or the programme itself lays the responsibility for coping with the job entirely at the door of the individual. The generalist nature of stress management groups makes it difficult for the needs of individual members to be met. This raises questions about the membership of such groups. How can its aims and objectives meet the needs of the individual member and the needs of the organization? Attending a stress management group may reveal difficulties which require one-to-one counselling. Reynolds and Briner (1996) argue that

> Stress Management Training provides healthy, non-distressed employees with a range of strategies and techniques which they can use to manage work demands. Worksite counselling and psychotherapy services aim to treat distressed individuals with a disorder or problem that may be irrelevant or peripheral to their work. (p. 146)

It is often difficult to distinguish how much a person's distress is due to work-related issues and how much to unrelated personal ones. They often overlap so that it is unclear which is cause and which is effect, for example, a client whose long-term relationship has ended is abusing alcohol and not coping at work. The relationship ended because of the long hours he had to work. His work is poor because of his drinking.

Six-session solution-focused stress management group

The workshop can be run in-house or draw its membership from a number of organizations. Prior to the group being convened potential members are asked to complete a questionnaire about their resources and strengths. They are invited to record their successful and their unsuccessful anti-stress strategies. They are asked to state what they would like to see happen in the group and how they hope to benefit from it.

Potential members are given information which covers the key, solution-focused ideas. It is made clear that the course is based upon the premise that individuals have some degree of responsibility for and control over their levels of stress. This is not to deny that organizations themselves may be 'sick' and in need of surgery to remove the causes of the stress they inflict upon their employees.

The course consists of eight one-and-a-half-hour sessions. It could be offered as a two-day course or spread over six separate sessions. If the latter the participants are given homework tasks to perform between sessions.

SESSION ONE

EXPECTATIONS AND GROUND RULES

- What do you hope will happen in this group?
- What do you hope will not happen?
- How will you know it has been successful?
- What will you/your customers/colleagues/people close to you notice is different about you if the course is successful?

On a scale of 0–10 with 10 being you are confident you will find this group helpful:

- Where are you on the scale?
- Is that high enough for you to feel positive or do you need to be higher?
- What would need to happen for that to happen?
- Do you have any ideas how the group could help you?

On another scale of 0–10 with 10 being you are willing to do virtually anything to make this group work and 0 is you intend to do as little as possible, where are you on the scale? Are you interested in moving up the scale?

- What do you think you will need to do to make this course work for you?
- What do you think you might need to do to make it work for the others?

Following discussion of these points, group members take a short period of time to write a personal and group learning contract. They state in positive, specific and behavioural terms what their personal goals are and how they will recognize progress towards them. They also negotiate ground rules for the group. These relate to:

- confidentiality
- commitment
- respect for course members and their goals
- resolving conflicts
- punctuality
- helpful and unhelpful behaviour.

The facilitators explain their role is not to be experts on people's problems but to draw out from group members their strengths, qualities and resources. They adopt a stance of curiosity as to how members make and sustain changes. They model to the group solution-focused values such as:

- respect for each client's ability to find a way through his or her problems
- the belief that the client has under-utilized potential
- empathy for the way the client sees the world
- curiosity as to how the client is dealing with his or her problem and what they might do in the future
- a non-expert stance which seeks to collaborate with the client.

SESSION TWO

DEFINING THE PROBLEM

In this session the facilitator leads a discussion on what stress is and how it affects different people. Stress may be externalized as a problem 'out there' which gets hold of people and influences them to think, feel and behave in certain ways. The task of the group is to find ways of recognizing the stress attack and reducing its sphere of influence. Individuals draw their own stress maps and share their concerns with another person in the group. The listening partner acknowledges the other's stress, explores what the stress means to the person and asks him or her questions about how they have and are coping with it. The person is asked to rate on a scale of 0–10 the degree of threat which the stress presents. The group's experiences of stress are shared and validated in the whole group.

The facilitator explains how people can create problems for themselves by:

- Adopting failed solutions.
- Erroneous thinking and holding irrational beliefs, for example, 'I must not make a mistake', 'I must be approved of by others all of the time'. Common cognitive distortions which lead to people making negative interpretations of events include:
  — excessive focusing on negatives to the exclusion of positives
  'Nothing good ever happens to me.'
  — discounting of achievements
  'I was lucky.'
  — either/or thinking
  'Either I am ecstatically happy or I am utterly miserable.'
  — all-or-nothing thinking
  'If I can't get exactly what I want I don't want anything.'
  — shoulds, oughts and musts.

By the end of this session participants are more aware of how they view and do stress as well as having some of their experiences normalized. At the same time they have begun to recognize their own and others' coping strategies. They are given the task of noticing times when they manage their stress better than others.

SESSION THREE

EXCEPTION SEEKING AND THE MIRACLE QUESTION

In this session participants are introduced to the idea there are exceptions to their stressful times. As exceptions are reported from the 'homework' task other memories of non-stress times are triggered off. Members are encouraged to become curious in their search for solutions. As members report exceptions and the strategies they used to make them happen, the facilitators compliment them on their discoveries.

The group is introduced to the miracle question:

Imagine if tonight when you were asleep a miracle happened and the problems which brought you to this group disappeared. But since you were asleep you did not know a miracle had happened. When you wake up how will you begin to find out a miracle has happened?

As the group explores its answer the facilitator makes the point that much of this can happen without waiting for a miracle. Some of it may have begun to happen already. Some of it the group could plan to work towards. Group members are encouraged to support each other in the exploration of their own miracle. This can best be done in pairs or triads. Homework will consist of choosing one small piece of the miracle which is attainable.

SESSION FOUR

AMPLIFYING CHANGE AND SCALING

Participants report further exceptions to the problem and successes in achieving small pieces of the miracle. The group is invited to pay compliments to each other. The facilitators ask questions to amplify the changes and to focus on how they were achieved. They explain the technique of scaling, first used in the introductory session. This time members explore how to use the scale of 0–10 to assess progress, confidence and motivation. They are invited to take one small step which will move them up one point on their scale. Their decision about which strategy to adopt is explored following the solution-focused principles of:

- If it is not broken do not fix it.
- If it works keep doing it.
- If it does not work stop doing it.
- Do something different.

SESSION FIVE

SOLUTIONS AND OTHERS

The facilitators continue to elicit more reports about change. They invite discussion about strategies for dealing with setbacks or lapses. Attention also focuses on the part others have to play in the members' lives. What do they notice is different about the members of the group? How do they scale them? What would they say the members' strengths and qualities are? How can others be allies in the search for solutions? The notion that small changes can lead to big changes in each member's interactional context is explained and discussed. The group may also be asked to apply to their own lives the acronym ECA:

Enjoy what you have
Change what you can
Accept what you must.

SESSION SIX

ENDING

Group members discuss and evaluate their progress in the group and explore how they could consolidate their gains. They may use scales to do this. Learning and maintenance questions (see Chapter 5) are used. Individuals make public personal learning statements which are affirmed and celebrated by others in the group. A call-back session within three months is a useful strategy for maintaining the impetus for change created by the group. Further needs individuals may have can be identified in this session.

Throughout the life of the group each member is encouraged to contribute. The facilitators build the group dynamics around invitations for others to comment upon the reports of others, with the proviso that comments must always be positive. Possible solutions are shared throughout. Ideally these ideas should be shared in a non-directive respectful manner but even when a group member is over-directive the person on the receiving end is asked, 'Of all the things John said what sounded most helpful to you? Did it give you any other ideas?' (Conlon, 2000).

Solution-focused groups possess a number of the factors identified by Yalom (1986) as important in group counselling:

1 The group instils hope.
2 It conveys to its members that they are not alone in their concerns.
3 It can release hidden or forgotten capacities for helping others.
4 It provides the opportunity for participants to learn and practise different ways of relating to others.
5 Group members can discover their own distinctive personal styles by watching the behaviour and listening to the ideas of others.
6 Membership enables cognitive and emotional understanding to develop.

Solution-focused stress groups are less stigmatizing than problem-focused ones as they teach skills which are of value to members in many aspects of their lives.

CHAPTER 8
Organizational Stress

It is estimated that 10 per cent of the UK's GNP is lost each year due to work-related stress in the form of sickness, staff turnover, lost production and increased selection costs (Arnold *et al.*, 1998).

The extent of employee stress in organizations has become a health and safety issue of considerable importance. A rising tide of successful employee litigation has prompted many organizations to evaluate the work pressures which make employees ill. Some organizations are themselves 'sick'. Their treatment of staff falls outside the healthy limits of pressure, challenge and competition. They try to avoid responsibility by placing the blame on the personal inadequacies of individual employees (if you can't stand the heat, don't come into the kitchen). But enlightened employers protect the mental health of their staff because they know that unless they do they will have high rates of sickness, poor performance and high staff turnover. Some employees, however, do bear a degree of responsibility for their part in allowing pressure to develop into stress. Some have personality traits inherited from their families of origin which make them more predisposed to stress. These might include: perfectionism, insecurity, desire to gain approval and lack of relationship-building skills among others. Employee responsibility extends to:

- Using the appropriate channels to discuss their work situation and to request change, for example, by having discussions with the line manager, implementation of complaints and grievance procedures and gaining the support of the relevant trade union if there is one.
- Seeking help for personal problems which are not associated with work.
- Developing the skills necessary to work effectively, for example, time management and IT skills.
- Making use of staff training and other resources or facilities open to them.
- Taking time off to recharge batteries and to restore the work/life balance.

Some employees will have found solutions which have become more part of the problem, for example, drinking heavily or working excessively. Through the support of an independent counsellor they can be helped to discard failed solutions and take whatever steps are available to them to reduce their stress. Counselling can help them to see where they have power to change, the resources to deal with challenges and the wisdom to accept what is beyond their control. It can help individuals to decide whether to stay within the organization and fight for a less stressful job or to leave and find one which will not harm them the way the present one does.

Stress is a product of the interaction between the organization and the employee. Neither may be wholly to blame. Each must accept responsibility for their part in the situation. Counsellors, whether they are in-house or employed by an outside agency, such as an Employee Assistance Programme, have a dual client relationship. The individual employee is their client but so also is the organization. The counsellor can feedback to the management what the sources of stress within the organization are. He or she can report its impact upon the workforce and highlight the need for structural change where appropriate. In some cases this may amount to identifying a particular employee who is creating a lot of stress for others or to draw attention to specific policies which are harmful to employees. Counsellors need to be wary that they are not drawn into taking the employee's side against the organization but, likewise, they must avoid colluding with management in the implementation of oppressive practices. For the counsellor there may be ethical dilemmas around a clash of values between counselling and the organization. As counselling and companies become more familiar with each other, there is perhaps less likelihood of this happening.

In this book I have followed Hobfoll's definition of stress (1998: 45). For him stress is

predicted to occur as a result of circumstances that represent (1) a threat of resource loss, or (2) actual loss of the resources required to sustain the individual-nested-in, family-nested-in social organization.

He predicted stress would occur when individuals did not receive reasonable gain for themselves or their social group from resource investment. Stress is never a 'good thing' even in moderation. Pressure can be. The following are organizational stressors which can threaten the individual employee:

- rising workloads and reductions in the number or quality of staff
- insufficient stability and security of employment
- an oppressive sick leave policy
- unrelenting (and often unproductive) change
- lack of information and consultation about change
- absence of clear and consistent policies
- erosion of pay and conditions of service
- insufficient time or training to enable people to feel skilled in their work – particularly in relation to new technology
- disregard for the employee's personal life – work/life balance
- unreasonable shift patterns
- a one-way demand for loyalty and commitment
- a failure to acknowledge or value the individual's contribution (negative appraisal)

- de-skilling of the employee through role conflict, ambiguity or over/underload
- banning of the informal procedures through which employees control their stress
- direct threats to the employee's status, income or prospects
- an unfair complaints procedure
- bullying
- sexist/racist/homophobic behaviour
- failure to support staff following a traumatic incident.

A specific form of employee stress is 'burn out'. Burn out is 'a syndrome of emotional exhaustion, depersonalisation and reduced personal accomplishment that can occur among individuals who do "people work" of some kind'(Maslach, 1982: 3). Sufferers lose their sense of care for their clients and become cynical, defeatist and disillusioned. They feel they have nothing left to give and experience a deep sense of failure. Their disillusionment may be associated with a lack of leadership in which there is little, if any, acknowledgement of how difficult their job is. The final straw may be a complaint or violence from a client. These individual experiences are compounded by a malaise in the work culture arising from the factors identified above. Another piece of the jigsaw is the social status of the work as reflected in the media and the political establishment.

It is often the most conscientious employees who become burnt out. Their loyalty and commitment to their clients make unreasonable demands upon their time and energy. Their adherence to high standards encourages them to push back the boundaries between life and work to such an extent that they live to work. The anxiety which drives this is likely to have its roots in early family patterns. This does not excuse organizations from their responsibility of care for those employees who need to be protected from themselves.

Although counselling can be deeply satisfying and rewarding, it also brings stresses on the counsellor. A counsellor has to contain distressing and traumatizing material brought by the client. Trauma counsellors have to hear and absorb stories of personal tragedy. On a daily basis counsellors witness the pain of people who have suffered horrendous abuse, loss and neglect. They are exposed to the full range of powerful human emotions, often in a raw form. They share the journey of people who are depressed, anxious, obsessed, lonely, fearful and suicidal. In the face of human suffering the counsellor often feels and is in fact powerless to help. Opportunities for the counsellor to discharge her or his own feelings are limited by confidentiality and may be restricted to a supervisor. There are additional factors which can lead to the work being stressful. These include: feeling unsafe in the counselling room with some clients; working beyond one's competence; poor caseload management skills and record keeping; ineffectual supervision, and working when ill or emotionally distracted. Without proof of successful outcomes the counsellor may also struggle to believe in the efficacy of the work itself.

Solution-focused workers frequently report that the values and spirit of the model have led to an increase in their job satisfaction. Many feel it has saved them from burn out. The reasons they put forward for this are:

- the balance between problem and solution talk energizes rather than drains the worker
- the increased level of client cooperation encourages the worker
- the evidence that the counselling is making a real difference to the client motivates and sustains the worker
- the practicality and elegant simplicity of the interventions increases the confidence of the worker
- having a consistent model increases competence and self-belief
- using the model with clients inevitably leads to applying its principles and techniques in the worker's personal life
- the optimism and hope imbedded in the model are infectious!

The solution-focused approach is not, however, a shield behind which the counsellor hides from the needs of clients. It should not be used as a form of avoiding the pain of the client in order to protect the counsellor. The counsellor is there primarily to meet the needs of the client. But having said that, counsellors also owe a duty of care towards themselves. They are responsible for their own mental health. This entails a careful monitoring of how they work. One form of support available to the counsellor under stress is supervision.

SUPERVISION

All professional counsellors are required to receive supervision for their work. The idea of a professional receiving supervision throughout his or her career can seem strange to an outsider. It does not imply incompetence. It is a commitment to ongoing professional development. Although not in itself a guarantee of good practice (some supervisors have low standards), in most cases it is a check on the quality of the counsellor's work. It serves as a form of protection for the client.

The roots of the solution-focused approach lie in a family therapy tradition which often uses live supervision. Members of a team view the counselling session through a two-way mirror and are able to telephone their ideas through to the counsellor or to hold a consultation break with him or her. At the break the team give the counsellor feedback on the session and may suggest points to raise with the client.

Solution-focused reflecting team

One form of group supervision is the reflecting team (Norman, 2000). There are six phases to the process:

PREPARATION

Those who will form the reflecting team are encouraged to think before the meeting what they would like to gain from the session.

PRESENTATION

The first person presents a case for the group's consideration.

CLARIFICATION

Following the presenter's outline of the case, any member of the group can ask questions to clarify issues. Questions which aim to do more than clarify are not allowed at this stage.

AFFIRMATION

Each member of the group feeds back to the presenter what he or she appreciated in the presentation. The presenter listens and acknowledges the feedback with a simple 'Thank you'.

REFLECTION

The members of the group take turns to make one response to the presentation. Contributors try to build upon previous contributions. The rounds of the group continue until everyone feels they have had their say. Members who feel they have nothing to say on a particular round say, 'Pass'. The presenter listens without comment throughout this stage.

CLOSURE

The presenter responds to what was discussed in the reflection phase. He or she may indicate which parts of the reflection were most relevant and helpful. The presenter may then say how he or she is thinking of using the feedback. The meeting continues with the next presenter.

These phases are parallel processes to those of solution-focused counselling itself. The reflecting team mirrors good solution-focused practice.

- It focuses on solutions and avoids hypothesizing about the problem.
- It looks for times when the counsellor was working well or was perceived as working well with the client.
- It assumes and validates the counsellor's strengths and resources.
- It aims to connect with the counsellor's unique style of working.
- It is respectful and collaborative.
- It does not regard itself as 'a panel of experts'.
- It does not concern itself with the right or the wrong way of viewing the case but offers multiple perspectives.
- It is not prescriptive but cooperative.

The egalitarian spirit of the reflecting team models good solution-focused practice. There is a clear congruence between the counselling and the supervision model being used. Group supervision enables individuals to learn how the model can be used differently in the hands of different people. The open nature of the group is a useful counterbalance to the prejudices and stereotypes an individual supervisee can be exposed to in one-to-one supervision. The group creates a climate of mutual respect in which they can celebrate skills, encourage creative ideas and learn from one another. Presenters report that the format allows them to listen, think about and choose what to use from the ideas discussed by the reflecting team. They can do this without feeling under pressure to respond immediately to interventions as one does in conventional group supervision. Even when the reflectors are off the mark in their observations they can help to increase the presenter's awareness of themselves. For example, the team speculated that the counsellor sounded as if she felt hopeless about work with a particular client but this remark only served to bring home to the presenter that she was actually hopeful and optimistic about this client. The fact that no one else believed this client could or would change made her realize how important it was that she remained hopeful about him.

Solution-focused counsellors, in common with all counsellors, need to be aware of how their own values and experiences, prejudices and stereotypes impact upon the therapeutic process. They need to be conscious of how they do or do not deal with stress in their own lives. Failure to do so may lead to a blurring of boundaries between the client's and the counsellor's material with resulting confusion, which in some circumstances can be exploitative. Solution-focused training courses do not compel trainees to undergo personal therapy. Many counsellors work in teams which offer live supervision of their work. Although this is very different from personal therapy it can act as a check on personal idiosyncrasies and biases. Video or audio recording of sessions is also very common even where teams are not used. As the British Association of Counselling and Psychotherapy acknowledges, personal development issues can be explored in many ways, not only through individual therapy. Professional and ethical counsellors make effective use of supervision and do not hesitate to use personal therapy when appropriate. They take care of themselves.

CRITICAL INCIDENT DEBRIEFING

Employees are increasingly being exposed to traumatic incidents at work. According to the American Psychiatric Association Diagnostic and Statistical Manual IV (1994) a traumatic incident is one where a person experiences or is witness to an event which involves actual or threatened death or serious injury or a threat to the physical integrity of the individual or others and the individual's response is one of intense fear, helplessness or horror. They are extraordinary events for which ordinary responses are inadequate. In the workplace these incidents may include: verbal intimidation; damage to property; physical threats or harassment; assaults and sexual offences including rape. They may take place in the context of a robbery, a theft or an attack of some kind. Employees may be held hostage or trapped for some time. As a consequence of such incidents employees may suffer varying degrees of post-traumatic stress. They may experience any or all of the following:

- guilt
- depression

- anxiety
- anger
- hyper vigilance/fear
- feeling overwhelmed
- disturbed sleep
- tearfulness
- irritability
- inability to settle or concentrate
- intrusive thoughts or flashbacks
- physical symptoms such as headaches
- feelings of isolation
- friction with people closest to them.

Some of these effects may be apparent immediately after the incident, others may not show themselves for months or even years. Not all employees require counselling following a traumatic incident. Some recover quickly and put it behind them. Others, however, are affected differently – perhaps due to their previous history, personality traits or social circumstances.

Critical Incident Debriefing (CID) is a structured exercise usually conducted in a group with all those affected by the incident present. It can also be done with individuals. In a debriefing people are given the opportunity with the help of a trained facilitator to explore their feelings, thoughts and actions in relation to the incident. According to Parkinson (1997) this airing helps the participants to make sense of their experiences and to 'normalize' their reactions. People are often ashamed and humiliated by their perceived failure to react 'better' at the time. The validation and acknowledgement of each person's experience will hopefully prevent future post-traumatic stress, although research on the efficacy of CID is not entirely convincing.

Employees often complain about the lack of care or understanding they received from employers following such incidents. The fact that a debriefing and counselling is offered to those who may need it is evidence the employer is taking their needs seriously. There may also be a need to make changes to make the working environment safer. The following solution-focused questions have been usefully employed as part of the planning for the future after a traumatic incident.

Miracle question

Alternative versions of the standard form of this question include:

1. Imagine you have been away on holiday and there has been an aggressive incident in the unit/office/shop and it has been well handled by the management. The workers felt supported and some strategies for making the place safer have been put into practice. What would your colleagues be telling you has happened to bring that about?
2. Imagine you are working in a safer environment in which you get adequate support: how are you thinking/feeling about work? What would you be doing differently or not doing? On your own? With others? What would be the signs that other people were doing things differently? Would the lay-out of the building or

anything else be different? What difference would this make to your clients, to your colleagues?

3. Imagine you have the skills necessary for dealing with aggressive, potentially violent clients. How did you get those skills? Where did you start?

Scaling

On a scale of 0-10, with 10 meaning you have the skills you need to deal with these incidents and 0 meaning you have none, where are you today? What would need to happen for you to move up just one point on the scale? Could you do this? When? How? What would need to happen for this to happen?

It is important to recognize that even with a high level of skills there is no guarantee that a critical incident will turn out to be anything other than an extremely frightening and stressful experience.

ORGANIZATIONAL CHANGE

Much of this book has been about what the individual could do to adapt to the stressful demands made upon them by their employers but employers also need to target the sources of stress which may be the product of faulty policies and procedures. According to Arnold *et al.* (1998) a healthy organization is one which is characterized by

> profitability and a physically and psychologically healthy workforce, which is able to maintain over time a healthy and satisfying work environment and organizational culture, particularly through periods of market turbulence and change.
>
> (p. 450)

The future orientation of the solution-focused approach fits well with the needs of organisations more interested in solutions than problems. The miracle question, for example, encourages staff to engage in fresh and imaginative thinking about the organisation without being lumbered with unnecessary baggage collected over the years. One version of it might be:

> If we came to work one day and the organization had changed overnight into the kind of organization we would like it to be, what would we notice was different?
> What would we or others be doing that was different?
> What would we or they have stopped doing?
> How would management, section heads, project leaders, the cleaners, the personnel department, administration, the finance department discover a miracle had happened?
> What difference would it make to them?
> How would our customers/clients know a miracle had happened?
> How would it have come about?
> What would have been the first thing that would have changed?
> What would need to happen for some of those things to happen?

Where would we start?
What would be the gains for various people?
Taking each example of change, on a scale of 0-10 where are we now in relation to making it happen?
Is that good enough?
Where do we want to get to?
How could we move up one point on the scale?
If one part of the organization had a piece of the miracle how would that affect other departments?   (adapted from O'Connell, 1998)

For organizations to create a working environment which is creative and productive but not stressful they need to:

- know what they do well
- do what they do well
- play to their strengths
- develop their strengths
- have clear goals and strategies which fit them
- manage change
- invest in training and staff support
- give credit to the right people and share rewards
- enable employees to progress
- build in variety to people's work
- allow for flexibility in employment practices – flexi-time/job sharing/maternity and paternity leave
- develop staff interpersonal/communication/team skills
- encourage employee participation
- decentralize and delegate wherever possible
- Give people control over their work as far as possible.

If organizations were able to develop such policies there would be little need for stress-management training and counselling.

APPENDIX
Solution-Focused Resources

There are many useful websites dedicated to the solution-focused and related approaches. Among them are the following sites, the locations of which were originally gathered together by Michael Durrant.

USA

http://www.brief-therapy.org/
http:// www.brief-therapy.org/hottips.htm
http://www.mri.org/
http://members.tripod.com/wjg45/SFBT/research.htm
http://www.solutionmind.com/solutiongroup/index.htm
http://brieftherapy.com/
http://www.talkingcure.com

AUSTRALIA

http://www.brieftherapysydney.com.au
http://www.stlukes.org.au

EUROPE

http://www.angelfire.com/biz/sikt/engindex.html
http://www.ebta.nu/
http://www.reteaming.com
http://www.nik.de/english/english.htm
http://www.fkc.se/index.htm
http://www.mckergow.com/

The sites include information about training opportunities. In the UK training is offered by:

The Brief Therapy Practice	Bill O'Connell
4d Shirland Mews	97 Glyn Farm Rd
London	Birmingham
W9 3DY	B32 1NJ
020 8968 0070	0121 422 2525

The University of Birmingham offers a Masters Course in Solution Focused Brief Therapy. For further information contact w.j.oconnell@bham.ac.uk

References

Aambo, A. (1997) 'Tasteful solutions: solution-focused work with groups of immigrants', *Contemporary Family Therapy* **19**(1): 63–79.

Abramowitz, S. I. and Murray, J. (1983) 'Race effects in psychotherapy', in J. Murray and P. R. Adamson (eds) *Bias in Psychotherapy*, New York: Praeger.

Adams, J. (1998) *Stress: A Friend for Life*, Saffron Walden: C. W. Daniel.

American Psychiatric Association (1994) Diagnostic and Statistical Manual of Mental Disorders, 4th revised edition, Washington: America Psychiatric Association.

Armstrong, J. (1999) 'Travelling hopefully', *The Therapist*, 6(1), Winter, pp. 14–17.

Arnold, J., Cooper, C. and Robertson, I. (1998) *Work Psychology, Understanding Human Behaviour in the Workplace*, London: *Financial Times* Management/Pitman.

Atkinson, D. R. (1985) 'Research on cross-cultural counselling and psychotherapy: a review and update of reviews', in P. Pederson (ed.) *Handbook of Cross Cultural Counselling and Psychotherapy*, New York: Praeger.

Bandler, R. and Grinder, J. (1979) *Frogs into Princes*, Moab, Utah: Real People Press.

Barret-Kruse, C. (1994) 'Brief counselling: a user's guide for traditionally trained counsellors', *International Journal for the Advancement of Counselling* 17: 109–15.

Berg, I. K. (1991) *Family Preservation: A Brief Therapy Workbook*, London: BT Press.

Berg, I. K. (1994) *Family Based Services*, New York: W. W. Norton.

Berg, I. K. and De Jong, P. (1996) 'Solution building conversations: co-constructing a sense of competence with clients', *Families in Society: The Journal of Contemporary Human Services*, June, pp. 376–91.

Berg, I. K. and Miller, S. (1992) *Working with the Problem Drinker: A Solution Focused Approach*, New York: W. W. Norton.

Boyd, A. (1999) *Life's Little Deconstruction Book*, London: Penguin.

British Association of Counselling (BAC) (1998) *Code of Ethics and Practice for Counsellors*, London: British Association of Counselling.

Burnham, J. (1986) *Family Therapy*, London: Tavistock.

Butler, W. R. and Powers, K. (1996) 'Solution focused grief therapy', in S. Miller, M. Hubble and B. Duncan (eds) *Handbook of Solution Focused Brief Therapy*, San Francisco: Jossey-Bass.

Carlson, R. (1997) *Don't Sweat the Small Stuff and It's All Small Stuff*, London: Hodder and Stoughton.

Colledge, S. (1999) 'Promoting Positive Parenting Project', Unpublished. Birmingham.

Conlon, S. (2000) 'Working with families and groups', Address to Midlands Association of Solution Focused Therapists.

Cramer, D. (1992) *Personality and Psychotherapy*, Milton Keynes: Open University Press.

Cullen, J. (1997) 'A pluralistic critique of brief solution-focused therapy', *The Social Worker* 65(1), Spring, pp. 1 and 6.

De Jong, P. and Hopwood, L. E. (1996) 'Outcome research on treatment conducted at the Brief Family Therapy Centre, 1992–3', in S. Miller, M. Hubble and B. Duncan (eds) *Handbook of Solution Focused Brief Therapy*, San Francisco: Jossey-Bass.

de Shazer, S. (1985) *Keys to Solutions in Brief Therapy*, New York: W. W. Norton.

de Shazer, S. (1988) *Clues: Investigating Solutions in Brief Therapy*, New York: W. W. Norton.

de Shazer, S. (1994) *Words were Originally Magic*, New York: W. W. Norton.

de Shazer, S. (1998a) *The Right Path or the Other Path?*, Brief Family Therapy Centre video. Milwaukee: Brief Therapy Practice.

de Shazer, S. (1998b) 'How come solution-focused brief therapists think diagnosis is so bad?', Brief Family Therapy Centre Milwaukee Internet site: www.brief-therapy.org

de Shazer, S. (1999) Personal communication.

de Shazer, S. and Berg, I. K. (1992) 'Doing therapy: a post-structural re-vision', *Journal of Marital and Family Therapy* 19: 121–4.

de Shazer, S. and Molnar, A. (1984) 'Four useful interventions in brief family therapy', *Journal of Marital and Family Therapy* 10(3): 297–304.

de Shazer, S., Berg, I. K., Lipchik, E., Nunnally, E., Molnar, A., Gingerich, W. and Weiner-Davis, M. (1986) 'Brief therapy: focused solution development', *Family Process* 25: 207–21.

Dolan, Y. (1991) *Resolving Sexual Abuse*, New York: W. W. Norton.

Dolan, Y. (1998) *One Small Step*, California: Papier-Mache Press.

Dryden, W. (ed.) (1992) *Integrative and Eclectic Therapy*, Buckingham: Open University Press.

Durrant, M. (1993) *Creative Strategies for School Problems*, Epping, New South Wales: Eastwood Family Therapy Centre.

Egan, G. (1990) *The Skilled Helper*, 4th edition, Belmont, CA: Brooks/Cole.

Egan, G. (1994) *The Skilled Helper*, 5th edition CA: Brooks/Cole.

Egan, G. (1998) *The Skilled Helper*, 6th edition, Belmont, CA: Brooks/Cole.

Erickson, M. H. (1980) *Collected Papers*, Vols 1–4 (ed. E. Rossi) New York: Irvington.

Feltham, C. (1997) 'Challenging the core theoretical model', *Counselling* 8(2): 121–5.

Frank, J. D. (1959) *American Journal of Psychotherapy* 115: 961–7.

Freedman, J. and Combs, G. (1993) 'Invitations to new stories: using questions to explore alternative possibilities', in S. Gilligan and R. Price *Therapeutic Conversations*, New York: Norton, pp. 291–303.

Freudenbeger, H. J. (1975) 'Theory, Research and Practice', *Psychotherapy* 12(1): 73–82.

Garfield, S. L. (1995) *Psychotherapy: An Eclectic–Integrative Approach*, Chichester: Wiley.

Garfield, S. L. and Bergin, A. E. (1994) *Handbook of Psychotherapy and Behavioural Change*, New York: Wiley.

George, E., Iveson, C. and Ratner, H. (1990) *Problem to Solution*, London: BT Press.

Gergen, K. J. (1999) *An Invitation to Social Construction*, London: Sage.

Gergen, K. J. and Gergen, M. J. (1986) 'Narrative form and the construction of psychological science', in T. R. Sabin (ed.) *Narrative Psychology: The Storied Nature of Human Conduct*, New York: Praeger.

Gilbey, G. and Turner, J. (1993) 'Use of the solution-focused model in groups', Unpublished.

Gilligan, S. and Price, R. (1993) *Therapeutic Conversations*, New York: W. W. Norton.

Gingerich, W. J. and Eisengart, S. (1999) 'Paper for the International Family Therapy Association, Akron, Ohio', 15 April.

Goddard, K. (1996) 'In defence of the past: a response to Ron Wilgosh Counselling', in S. Palmer, S. Dainow and P. Milner (eds) *The BAC Counselling Reader*, London: Sage, pp. 408–11.

Hales, J. (1999) 'Person centred counselling and solution-focused therapy', *Counselling*, August, 10(3): 233–6.

Hawkes, D., Marsh, T. I. and Wilgosh, R. (1998) *Solution Focused Therapy – A Handbook for Health Care Professionals*, Oxford: Butterworth-Heinemann.

Heaton, J. (1972) 'Insight in phenomenology and psychoanalysis', *Journal of the British Society of Phenomenology* 3: 135.

Hobfoll, S. E. (1998) *Stress, Culture, and Community – The Psychology and Philosophy of Stress*, New York: Plenum Press.

Honey, P. and Mumford, A. (1992) *The Manual of Learning Styles*, Maidenhead: A. Mumford.

Hudson, P. and O'Hanlon, W. (1991) *Rewriting Love Stories*, New York: W. W. Norton.

Janis, I. (1983) *Short-term Counselling, Guidelines on Recent Research*, New Haven: Yale University Press.

Kelly, G. A. (1955) *The Psychology of Personal Constructs*, New York: W. W. Norton.

Korman, H. (1997) 'On the ethics of constructing realities', *Contemporary Family Therapy* 19(1): 105–15.

Koss, M. P. and Butcher, J. N. (1986) 'Research on brief therapy', in S. L. Garfield and A. E. Begin (eds) *Handbook of Psychotherapy and Behaviour Change*, 3rd edition, New York: Wiley.

Kral, R. and Kowalski, K. (1989) 'After the miracle: the second stage in solution-focused brief therapy', *Journal of Strategic and Systemic Therapies* 8(2): 73–6.

Kushner, H. (1986) *When All You've Ever Wanted Isn't Enough*, London: Pan.

Lambert, M. J. and Bergin, A. E. (1994) 'The effectiveness of psychotherapy', in A. E. Bergin and S. L. Garfield *Handbook of Psychotherapy and Behaviour Change*, 4th edition, New York: J. Wiley.

Lawson, D. (1994) 'Identifying pre-treatment change'. *Journal of Counselling and Development*, 72: 244–8

Lazarus, A. (1981) *The Practice of Multi Modal Therapy*, New York: McGraw-Hill.

Lee, M. Y., Greene, G. J. and Rheinscheld, J. (1999) 'A model for short-term solution-focused group treatment of male domestic violence offenders', *Journal of Family Social Work* 3(2): 39–57.

Lipchick, E. and de Shazer, S. (1986) 'The purposeful interview', *Journal of Strategic and Family Therapies* 5(1): 88–9.

Lipchick, E. and Kubicki, A. (1996) 'Solution focused domestic violence views', in S. Miller, M. Hubble and B. Duncan *Handbook of Solution Focused Brief Therapy*, San Francisco: Jossey-Bass.

Lomas, P. (1987) *The Limits of Interpretation*, London: Penguin.

McDonald, A. J. (1994) 'Brief therapy in adult psychiatry', *Journal of Family Therapy* 16: 415–526.

McKeel, A. and Weiner-Davis, M. (1995) 'Pre-suppositional questions and pre-treatment change: a further analysis', Unpublished.

McLeod, J. (1997) *Narrative and Psychotherapy*, London: Sage.

McLoughlin, B. (1995) *Developing Psychodynamic Counselling*, London: Sage.

McNamee, S. and Gergen, K. J. (1992) *Therapy as Social Construction*, Newbury Park, CA: Sage.

Mahoney, M. J. and McRay-Patteson, K. (1992) 'Changing theories of change', in S. Brown, and R. Lent (eds) *Handbook of Counselling Psychology,*. New York: J. Wiley.

Maslach, C. (1982) *Burn Out – The Cost of Caring*, New York: Prentice Hall Press.

Metcalf, L. (1997) *Parenting Towards Solutions*, Englewood Cliffs, NJ: Prentice Hall.

Metcalf, L., Thomas, F. N., Duncan, B. L, Miller, S. D. and Hubble, M. A. (1996) 'What works in solution-focused brief therapy', in S. D. Miller, M. A. Hubble and B. L. Duncan (eds) *Handbook of Solution-Focused Brief Therapy*, San Francisco: Jossey-Bass.

Miller, G. (1997) *Becoming Miracle Workers*, New York: Walter de Gruyter.

Miller, S. D., Duncan, B. L. and Hubble, M. (1997) *Escape from Babel – Towards a Unifying Language of Psychotherapy Practice*, New York: W. W. Norton.

Miller, S. D., Hubble, M. A. and Duncan, B. L. (eds) (1996) *Handbook of Solution Focused Brief Therapy*, San Francisco: Jossey-Bass.

Milner, P. and Palmer, S. (1998) *Integrative Stress Counselling*, London: Cassell.

Nelson-Jones, R. (2000) 'Creating counselling and therapy theories', *Counselling* 11(1): 10–13.

Norman, H. (2001) 'Reflecting teams', Unpublished. Paper presented at the Midland Association for Solution Focused Therapy, February.

O'Connell, B. (1998) *Solution Focused Therapy*, London: Sage.

O'Hanlon, B. and Beadle, S. (1994) *A Field Guide to Possibility Land: Possibility Therapy Methods*, Omaha, NB: Possibility Press.

Palmer, S. (1990) 'Stress mapping: a visual technique to aid counselling and training.' *Counselling Today* (2): 9–12.

Palmer, S. and Woolfe, R. (2000) *Integrative and Eclectic Psychotherapy*, London: Sage.

Parkinson, F. 1997) *Critical Incident Debriefing: Understanding and Dealing with Trauma*, London: Souvenir Press.

Paul, G. L. (1966) *Insight versus Desensitization in Psychotherapy*, California: Starford University Press.

Pekarik, G. and Wierzbicki, J. (1986) 'The relationship between clients' expected and actual treatment duration', *Journal of Clinical Child Psychology* 23: 121–5.

Perry, W. (1970) *Forms of Intellectual and Ethical Development in the College Years: a Schema*, New York: Rinehart and Winston.

Piaget, J. (1954) *The Construction of Reality in the Child*, New York: Basic Books.

Prochaska, J. O., Di Clemente, C. C. and Norcross, J. C. (1992) 'In search of how people change', *American Psychologist* 47, 1102–14.

Reynolds, S. and Briner, R. B. (1996) 'Stress management at work: with whom, for whom and to what ends?', in S. Palmer and W. Dryden (eds) *Stress Management and Counselling*, London: Cassell.

Rogers, C. R. (1961) *On Becoming a Person: A Therapist's View of Psychotherapy*, London: Constable.

Rosenbaum, R., Hoyt, M. and Talmon, M. (1990) 'The challenge of single session therapies: creating pivotal moments', in R. Wells and V. Gianetti (eds) *The Handbook of Brief Therapies*, New York: Plenum.

Santa Rita Jr, E. (1998) 'What do you do after asking the miracle question in solution-focused therapy?', *Family Therapy* 25(3): 189–95.

Selekman, M. (1991) 'The solution-oriented parenting group: a treatment alternative that works', *Journal of Strategic and Systemic Therapies* 10(1): 36–48.

Selekman, M. (1997) *Solution Focused Therapy with Children*, New York: The Guilford Press.

Sloane, R. B., Staples, F. R., Cristol, A. H., Yorkson, N. J. and Wipple, K. (1975) *Psychotherapy versus Behaviour Therapy*, Cambridge, MA: Harvard University Press.

Smail, D. (1987) *Taking Care: An Alternative to Therapy*, London: Dent.

Smith, M., Glass, G. and Miller, T. (1980) *The Benefits of Psychotherapy*, Baltimore: Johns Hopkins University Press.

Talmon, M. (1990) *Single Session Therapy*, San Francisco: Jossey-Bass.

Tedeschi, R. G., Park, C. and Calhoun, L. (1999) *Post-traumatic Growth: Positive Changes in the Aftermath of Crisis*, Mahwah, New Jersey: LEA.

Turnell, A. and Edwards, S. (1999) *Signs of Safety – A Solution and Safety Oriented Approach to Child Protection Casework*, New York: W. W. Norton.

Van Deurzen-Smith, E. (1988) *Existential Counselling in Practice*, London: Sage.

Washburn, P. (1994) 'Advantages of a brief solution oriented focus in home based family preservation services', *Journal of Systemic Therapies* 13(2): 47–57.

Watzlawick, P. (1984) *The Invented Reality*, New York: W. W. Norton.

Watzlawick, P., Weakland, J. and Fisch, R. (1974) *Change: Principles of Problem Formation and Problem Resolution*, New York: W. W. Norton.

Weakland, J., Fisch, R., Watzlawick, P. and Bodin, A. (1974) 'Brief therapy: focused problem solution', *Family Processes* 13: 141–68.

Weiner-Davis, M., de Shazer, S. and Gingerich, W. (1987) 'Building on pre-treatment change to construct the therapeutic solution: an exploratory study', *Journal of Marital and Family Therapy* 13(4): 359–63.

Wells, R. and Gianetti, V. (eds) (1993) *Casebook of the Brief Psychotherapies*, New York: Plenum Press.

White, M. (1989) *Selected Papers*, Adelaide: Dulwich Centre Publications.

White, M. (1993) 'Deconstruction and therapy', in S. Gilligan and R. Price (eds) *Therapeutic Conversations*, New York: W. W. Norton.

White, M. and Epston, D. (1990) *Narrative Means to Therapeutic Ends*, New York: W. W. Norton.

Wilgosh, R. (1993) 'How can we see where we're going if we're always looking backwards?', *Counselling* 4(2): 98–101.

Yalom, I. D. (1986) *The Theory and Practice of Group Psychotherapy*, New York: Basic Books.

Zeig, J. K. and Munion, W. M. (1999) *Milton H. Erickson*, London: Sage.

Zimmerman, T. S., Prest, L. A. and Wetzel, B. E. (1997) 'Solution focused couple therapy groups: an empirical study', *Journal of Family Therapy* 19: 125–44.

Index